PROJECT PARADIGM

AN ARCHETYPE FOR TRANSITIONING INDIVIDUALS AND ORGANIZATIONS TO PROJECTIZATION

FRANK BISBIGLIA MPM, PMP

CONTENTS

NOTES
CORE KNOWLEDGE FOR A PROJECTIZED WORLD

NOTES
CASEWORK FROM NASA'S ADVANCED SUPERCOMPUTING (NAS)

NOTES
LEADING THE WORK

NOTES
THE PLAYBOOK

NOTES
LEADING THE WORK

REFERENCES

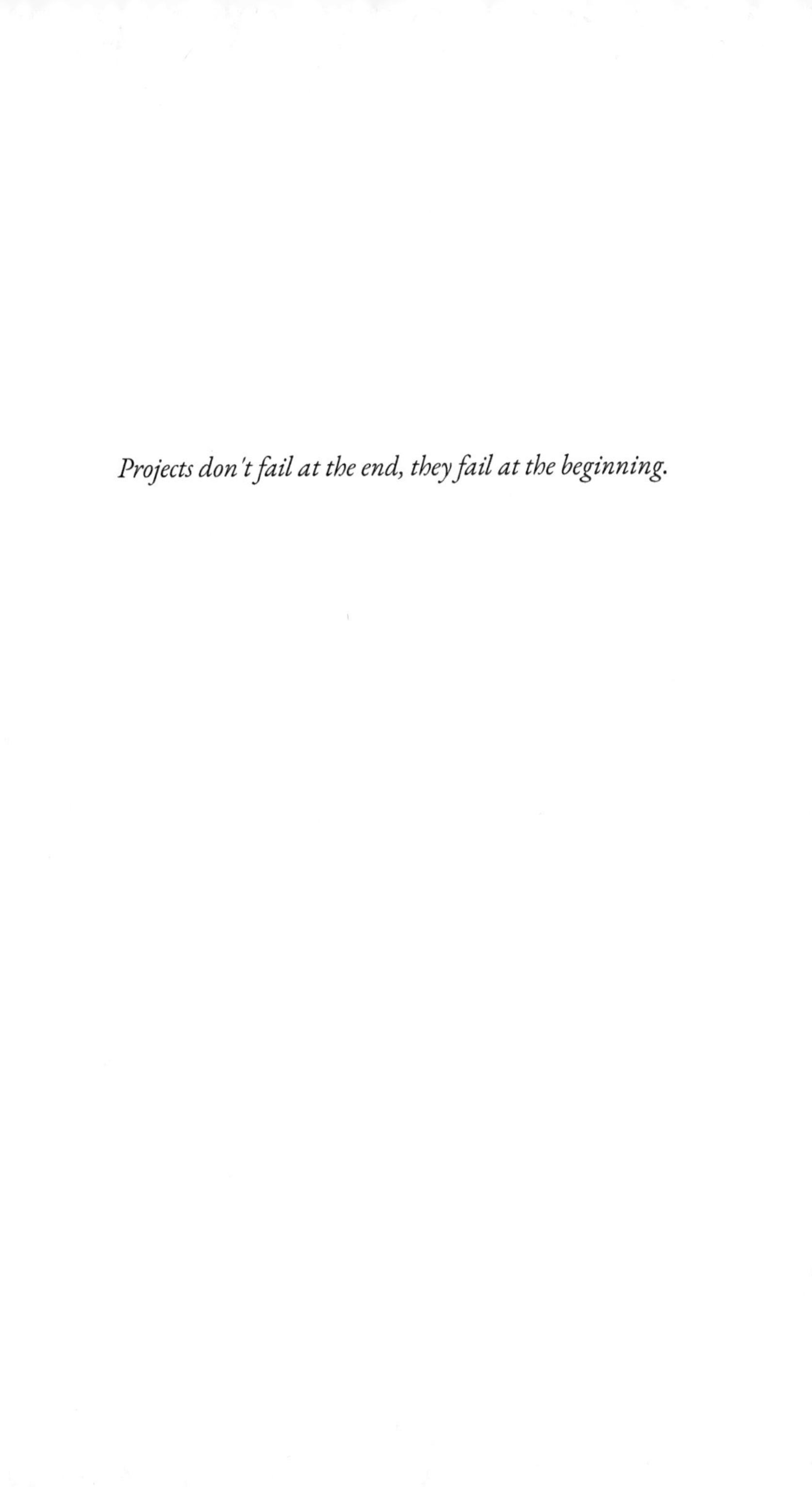

Projects don't fail at the end, they fail at the beginning.

INTRODUCTION
THE WEIGHT OF CHANGE

As Marty McFly would say to Doc in the movie *Back to the Future*, "That's heavy, Doc."

Change is one of the most unsettling experiences human beings face. It disrupts routines, threatens identity, and exposes us to uncertainty. Most people don't simply resist change; they dread it. A familiar job, even if unfulfilling, feels safer than a new opportunity. An established process, even if inefficient, feels less risky than an untested innovation. Psychologists call this the status quo bias, our tendency to prefer the known over the unknown, even when the unknown might benefit us.

LEADERSHIP AND OWNERSHIP IN UNCERTAIN TIMES

"Leadership in moments of change requires more than skill; it requires ownership." As Jocko Willink writes in *Extreme Ownership*, leaders must "own everything in their world," including problems, failures, and uncertainties. By taking responsibility rather than blaming external factors, individuals and teams build the trust and resilience needed to face the unknown.

Richard Branson echoes a similar philosophy. Known for his boldness at Virgin, Branson has often said that "business opportunities are like buses, there's always another one coming." That statement isn't just optimism; it reflects a mindset of fluid adaptation. Branson built an empire not by clinging to rigid structures but by embracing change as an operating principle. He has openly admitted that many of his ventures started with imperfect information but moved forward because "the worst thing you can do is do nothing."

Where Willink focuses on personal accountability, Branson focuses on the cultural permission to try, fail, and pivot. Both leaders are describing two sides of the same truth: change demands movement. Leadership is what transforms hesitation into action.

CHANGE IS THE ONLY CONSTANT

The irony is that change is not optional. It is the only constant in modern life. Technology evolves. Markets shift. Generations redefine what work and meaning look like. Jordan Peterson notes that humans derive stability from order, but growth requires venturing into chaos, the unfamiliar, the uncomfortable, and the unpredictable. In the world of work, this means embracing change not as a passing storm but as the permanent climate.

Willink frames leadership as the anchor amid chaos. Leaders don't eliminate uncertainty; they navigate it, setting the example for others. When leaders demonstrate calm ownership in the face of volatility, they permit their teams to step forward, not shrink back.

Jeff Bezos has expressed a similar sentiment in one of his annual shareholder letters, writing that "Staying in Day 1 mode means you're never done, **never comfortable**, never standing still. If we become complacent, it's Day 2: stasis, followed by irrelevance, followed by excruciating, painful decline, followed by death." For Bezos, the most dangerous thing an organization can do is assume the world will stand still. Change is the default setting, not the exception.

That ethos shaped Amazon's organizational DNA: an obsession with customers, a willingness to experiment relentlessly, and a comfort operating in ambiguity. Bezos's insight is particularly relevant to the project-based economy, where organizations can no longer rely on static hierarchies or long strategic planning cycles. Instead, they must continuously iterate, learn, and redeploy resources wherever value emerges.

THE HUMAN FEAR BEHIND ORGANIZATIONAL SHIFTS

When organizations restructure around projects rather than fixed hierarchies, it can feel destabilizing. The old guarantees of lifetime employment and predictable benefits begin to vanish. For individuals, this shift sparks fear:

"Will I still belong?"

"Will I still be able to provide for my family?"

"Will I be good enough?"

Being out of work is a kind of quiet shock that settles into your chest before you even know what to do with it. There's an emptiness that hits you in waves—this sense of What now? and Why me? And no matter how many times you replay the events leading up to it, none of it feels fair. It feels messed up, like the rug was pulled with no warning, and suddenly you're sitting alone trying to figure out how to explain something you still don't fully understand yourself. How do I tell my wife without feeling like I've let her down? Should I tell my son, or pretend everything is fine so he doesn't worry? Do I tell friends, or keep it to myself so I don't have to see that look in their eyes—the mix of sympathy and curiosity about what really happened? And what story do I tell the outside world, the people who ask casually, "How's work?" as if the answer isn't gut-wrenching?

Then there are the practical questions that pile up fast: What do I say to potential employers about why I'm not working? How do I sound honest without sounding damaged? Do I start firing off resumes immediately, or take time to breathe and figure out what I actually want next? How do I keep myself from slipping into laziness or anxiety in the space between roles? Do I have enough money saved to float me until something else comes through? What about the mortgage? Health insurance? It all hits at once: the fear, the uncertainty, the sudden pressure to rewrite your future on the fly.

But somewhere within all that chaos is the harder, quieter work—finding your path again, finding the courage to stay calm, and reminding yourself that this moment, as brutal as it feels, doesn't define who you are or what you've built. It sucks. It's gut-wrenching. But it's also a transition, not an ending, and you're allowed to navigate it one honest step at a time.

These are not abstract worries; they are deeply human anxieties tied to survival and identity. Anthropologists note that stability and predictability have been central to how humans structure their societies. When those pillars wobble, fear and resistance naturally follow.

Eric Schmidt, former CEO of Google and co-author of *Trillion Dollar Coach*, argues that great leaders create psychological safety through clarity, not false certainty. He describes how Bill Campbell guided teams through Google's hypergrowth by acknowledging uncertainty while reinforcing shared purpose and trust. "Leaders can't promise stability," Schmidt notes, "but they can promise that the team will face instability together." This is a critical leadership distinction: you don't need to eliminate uncertainty; you need to create clarity of direction and unity of movement in its presence.

This leadership stance mirrors Bezos's "Day 1" philosophy and Branson's bold experimentation. Change becomes less threatening when people believe they are part of something adaptive, resilient, and shared.

FROM FEAR TO OPPORTUNITY

History repeatedly demonstrates that those who embrace change are not merely survivors; they become the architects of their own success. As Lee Iacocca once said, "Apply yourself. Get all the education you can, but then, by God, do something. Don't just stand there, make it happen." This call to action captures a fundamental truth: the discomfort of change is real, but so is the extraordinary opportunity it can unlock.

Richard Branson's career is a testament to this principle. He did not have a single linear career path; instead, he jumped from records to airlines to space travel, constantly exploring new opportunities others saw as risky. He has said, "You don't learn to walk by following rules. You learn by doing and by falling over." That statement isn't just entrepreneurial bravado; it's a model for personal and organizational resilience in the face of change.

In Amazon's case, Bezos turned the fear of being disrupted into a cultural driver: "Your margin is my opportunity," he famously said, signaling that disruption is both inevitable and exploitable. Amazon's ability to thrive came from embedding change into its operating structure, small, autonomous teams (the "two-pizza team" model), rapid iteration, and an obsessive focus on delivering value faster than the competition.

Eric Schmidt saw something similar at Google. Under his leadership, Google scaled not by controlling change but by embracing distributed leadership, allowing teams to experiment, learn, and move quickly. Google's model wasn't built to avoid disruption; it was built to harness it.

EDUCATION AS A CATALYST, NOT A SHELTER

In today's rapidly evolving landscape, education must be understood in its broadest sense. It is no longer confined to traditional classrooms or formal degree programs. Training, certifications, apprenticeships, micro-credentials, and project-based learning are redefining how individuals acquire and apply knowledge. In fact, as Michael Gibson emphasizes in *Paper Belt on Fire*, traditional education systems are themselves undergoing a profound transformation, one that rewards initiative, adaptability, and practical application over **rote credentialing**.

Bezos has also underscored this idea. He once remarked, "People who are right a lot, they listen a lot. They also change their minds a lot. If you don't change your mind frequently, you're going to be wrong a lot." This mindset of constant learning, listening, and adapting is core to thriving in a world where knowledge has a shorter half-life than ever before.

Branson similarly encourages a bias toward action over credentialism: "You don't need to be a rocket scientist. If you've got a good idea, go out and do it." He has built multiple businesses by empowering people without elite degrees but with an entrepreneurial spirit and a clear nod to the value of adaptability over pedigree.

LEADERSHIP THAT MOVES AWARENESS INTO ACTION

This shift means that the most successful individuals are those who not only learn but act decisively on that learning. They invest in developing new skills, experiment boldly, and leverage their knowledge to create value in emerging industries and unconventional spaces. Change may unsettle, but for those prepared to engage it, change is also the gateway to relevance, leadership, and sustained impact.

"Extreme ownership transforms knowledge into action. Leaders set the tone: they don't wait for perfect clarity, they move forward with discipline and adaptability. In project-driven environments, this kind of leadership inspires others to act rather than freeze in uncertainty."

Eric Schmidt emphasizes a similar principle: leaders must empower teams to act rather than over-control them. When facing uncertainty, over-analysis can paralyze. Decentralized decision-making, coupled with a clear vision, allows organizations to adapt faster than competitors.

Branson's approach to leadership is famously informal, but deeply strategic: trust people, empower them, and be ready to adjust course quickly. He has said, "If somebody offers you an amazing opportunity and you're not sure you can do it, say yes —then learn how to do it later." That ethos is rooted in the belief that action precedes certainty, not the other way around.

OWNING THE SHIFT

This book begins from that tension. Change is hard. It always has been. But in today's project-based economy, resisting change is no longer a safe option. The organizations and individuals who face it honestly, who admit the fear, but prepare with skill and discipline, will be the ones who turn disruption into advantage.

Richard Branson reminds us that embracing risk opens doors to innovation.

Jeff Bezos warns that standing still is the beginning of decline.

Eric Schmidt teaches that leadership means giving clarity in uncertain times.

Each of these leaders, in their own way, demonstrates that successful navigation of change isn't about eliminating risk. It's about owning the process, adapting continuously, and creating momentum where others freeze.

CHANGE AS LEADERSHIP'S DEFINING MOMENT

The Project Paradigm is about facing this challenge head-on. It provides tools, stories, and practices to help professionals and families navigate the shift from permanence to projects. It acknowledges the dread of change but insists on the possibility of transformation.

"Leadership is the force that moves awareness into action."

In Willink's words, "There are no bad teams, only bad leaders."

Whether in a family, a project team, or an entire organization, leadership is what turns uncertainty into coordinated movement. Awareness is the first step. Action is the second.

PART ONE
THE SHIFT

O

THE PROJECT-BASED ECONOMY

The world of work is undergoing a quiet revolution. Across industries as diverse as aerospace, retail, finance, healthcare, entertainment, and government, projects—not permanent jobs—are becoming the primary units of value delivery. This is more than a buzzword trend. It is a fundamental rewiring of how organizations create, capture, and sustain competitive advantage.

FROM JOBS TO MISSIONS

For most of the 20th century, a career meant a stable employer, a fixed role, and a ladder you climbed over the course of decades. Job descriptions were designed to be broad enough to survive economic cycles, technological shifts, and management reshuffles. Today, the default is shifting from roles to missions: bounded, time-limited efforts with a clear purpose, measurable outcomes, and cross-functional teams.

Guy Standing, in *The Precariat* (2011), warned that "the 20th century income and labor security model is giving way to a landscape of short-term contracts and contingent work." He framed this not just as an economic shift but as a psychological challenge, workers facing uncertainty about identity, stability, and long-term security. What Standing described as a risk can also be seen as an opportunity if individuals learn to operate like project entrepreneurs: flexible, skilled, and portfolio-minded.

Stephen Covey's classic *7 Habits of Highly Effective People* (1989) provides a mindset blueprint. Covey's first habit, "Be Proactive," speaks directly to today's project economy. **No one** is coming to design your career for you; you must take ownership, define your "circle of influence," and actively shape your next assignment. Covey's emphasis on beginning with the end in mind resonates with project charters: every mission needs a vision, a definition of done, and a purpose that motivates people to act.

WHY PROJECTS ARE WINNING

Several forces explain the staying power of projectization.

1. Coordination Costs Have Collapsed

Digital platforms have destroyed the friction that once made large, permanent organizations necessary. Collaboration suites like Microsoft Teams, Slack, Zoom, and Asana allow a geographically dispersed team to align in hours, not weeks. AI tools now draft meeting notes, detect scheduling risks, and summarize long documents in seconds. In Lee Iacocca's words from *Where Have All the Leaders Gone?* (2007), "We are continually faced with great opportunities brilliantly disguised as insoluble problems." Lower friction turns what used to be insoluble, rapidly forming, high-performing teams, into an everyday practice.

2. Volatility Rewards Agility

Markets move faster than static org charts. When customer expectations, regulations, or technology shift overnight, project structures allow leaders to pivot resources quickly. Iacocca built Chrysler's turnaround in the late 1970s on "fast action teams" empowered to make decisions without waiting for endless approvals. He believed speed was a competitive weapon and famously said, "The ability to concentrate and to use your time well is everything." Projects are built for that concentration.

3. Talent Wants Flexibility

Millennials and Gen Z value autonomy and variety more than titles and corner offices. Surveys consistently show that younger workers are comfortable assembling a portfolio career, consulting, teaching, launching side ventures, and freelancing if it provides growth and purpose. James Altucher, in *Choose Yourself* (2013), argues that "no one is going to pick you" in this economy; you must create your own opportunities and multiple income streams. Project work, by its nature, offers exactly that: discrete assignments where you can prove value, learn new skills, and move to the next adventure.

4. Economics Favor Variable Capacity

For organizations, funding work as projects aligns costs with value increments. Instead of carrying large, fixed payrolls, companies can flex capacity up or down. This is especially attractive in technology, where product cycles are short and market timing is critical. As Kory Kogon and Suzette Blakemore explain in *Project Management for the Unofficial Project Manager* (2015), leaders are under pressure to "do more with less, deliver faster, and delight customers," even when formal project structures don't exist. Projectization offers a disciplined way to meet those demands without bloated overhead.

CAREER IMPLICATIONS: YOUR RÉSUMÉ BECOMES A PORTFOLIO

In a project economy, your career narrative shifts from title progression to proof of impact. Instead of saying, "I was a Senior Analyst at Company X for five years," the more powerful story is, "I led a cross-functional initiative that reduced data-processing time by 40 percent and trained two successor teams." Each project becomes a case study in leadership, problem-solving, and value creation.

Altucher's advice to "become an idea machine" aligns perfectly here. Each project you join or launch yourself becomes a laboratory to test ideas, learn fast, and capture stories that demonstrate resilience. Think of your LinkedIn profile not as a list of employers but as a portfolio of missions accomplished: charters authored, risks mitigated, products launched, systems migrated, communities built.

Kogon and Blakemore emphasize that even if you don't carry the title of "Project Manager," the skill set is non-negotiable. Their book champions the "unofficial project manager," the marketer, engineer, nurse, or analyst who must still define scope, manage stakeholders, and communicate status. In today's workplace, everyone is a project manager at some point.

ORGANIZATIONAL IMPLICATIONS: VALUE FLOWS THROUGH PORTFOLIOS

For leaders, the takeaway is equally clear: manage portfolios, not just departments. Projects are the arteries through which value flows. Metrics such as throughput, forecast accuracy, and stakeholder satisfaction become more meaningful than headcount or budget alone.

Lee Iacocca's turnaround at Chrysler provides a master class. Facing bankruptcy, he created a portfolio of critical initiatives, including new models, cost-reduction programs, and government negotiations. Iacocca measured each against aggressive milestones. "In times of great stress or adversity," he wrote, "it's always best to keep busy, to plow your anger and your energy into something positive." The discipline of portfolio management channels that energy into visible outcomes.

Modern PMOs (Project Management Offices) reflect this philosophy. Rather than heavy bureaucracies, effective PMOs act as lightweight governance hubs: they standardize charters, maintain dependency maps, and provide leaders with real-time visibility into risk and progress. The goal is transparency without throttling creativity.

THE HUMAN SIDE OF THE SHIFT

Guy Standing's concept of "the precariat" reminds us that projectization carries a **human cost**. Income volatility, lack of benefits, and constant reskilling pressure can breed anxiety. Covey's habit of "Sharpen the Saw"—regularly renewing your physical, mental, and emotional capacity—is not just self-help fluff; it's a survival strategy. Professionals must cultivate networks, maintain emergency funds, and invest in lifelong learning to navigate gaps between projects.

Organizations share responsibility. Companies that embrace project-based models should offer portable benefits, invest in knowledge capture to reduce turnover risk, and treat contractors with dignity. Projects succeed when people feel safe to speak up, challenge assumptions, and contribute ideas. As Kogon and Blakemore note, "people drive projects, not processes."

NASA as a Living Example

NASA's Advanced Supercomputing (NAS) Division illustrates this shift. Historically operations-centric, NAS increasingly relies on project charters to launch new HPC clusters, integrate GPU nodes, and upgrade data services. Instead of relying solely on permanent roles, NAS forms temporary cross-disciplinary teams of engineers, scientists, procurement specialists, and security experts to deliver specific outcomes. The result is greater predictability, faster decision cycles, and a culture that rewards measurable progress.

ACTION TAKEAWAYS

For Individuals

- Think in missions. Frame every assignment, no matter your title, as a project with a charter, milestones, and lessons learned.
- Document value. Capture metrics and stories from each project to include in your portfolio.
- Invest in adaptability. Build skills in communication, risk management, and scheduling that transfer across industries.

For Organizations

- Fund outcomes. Shift budgeting from departments to projects with clear deliverables.
- Enable talent liquidity. Create internal marketplaces where employees can bid on or volunteer for projects.
- Measure what matters, track throughput, forecast accuracy, and stakeholder satisfaction over activity hours.

As Lee Iacocca often reminded his teams, "The discipline of writing something down is the first step toward making it happen." In a project-based economy, the discipline that charters the vision, scopes the work, and communicates the plan is the difference between chaos and progress.

KEY TAKEAWAYS

1. The Nature of Work Is Fundamentally Changing

- Permanent roles are giving way to projects as the primary units of value delivery.
- This shift is reshaping how individuals build careers and how organizations create advantage.
- Project work enables speed, focus, and flexibility in volatile markets.

2. Individuals Must Think in Missions, Not Titles

- Careers are evolving from hierarchical job ladders to portfolios of completed missions.
- Success depends on adaptability, communication, and the ability to lead without formal authority.

- Professionals who document their impact and grow their project management skills will thrive.

3. Organizations Must Evolve Their Operating Models

- Value flows through project portfolios, not traditional departmental structures.
- Lean PMOs and lightweight governance help align strategy, execution, and accountability.
- Effective leaders fund outcomes, not headcount, and measure throughput, accuracy, and stakeholder satisfaction.

4. Technology Enables, but Culture Sustains, Projectization

- Collaboration and AI tools lower coordination costs and speed up delivery.
- Trust, transparency, and a shared sense of purpose remain the foundation of effective project work.

5. The Human Factor Cannot Be Ignored

- The shift to project-based work brings uncertainty, income variability, and constant upskilling.
- Individuals need resilience strategies, networks, savings, and continuous learning.
- Organizations must support this new reality through portable benefits, psychological safety, and respect for contributors.

6. Leadership Is About Action

- As Jack Welch said, "Good business leaders create a vision, articulate the vision, passionately own the vision, and relentlessly drive it to completion."
- In a project economy, leadership means turning vision into clear missions, empowering people, and enabling teams to deliver measurable outcomes.

1

WHY NOW? TECHNOLOGY, ECONOMICS, AND DEMOGRAPHICS

Why is the shift toward a project-based economy happening now? The answer lies in the convergence of three powerful forces: technology, economics, and demographics. Each of these forces reinforces the others, creating a self-accelerating cycle of change.

TECHNOLOGY: ACCELERATION WITHOUT BORDERS

The digital transformation of the last decade has dramatically lowered the cost and friction of collaboration. What once required large, co-located teams and expensive infrastructure can now be executed by small, distributed networks of professionals across time zones. Cloud platforms such as Microsoft Azure, AWS, and Google Cloud allow teams to spin up environments in minutes rather than months, democratizing access to computing power that was once the exclusive domain of large enterprises.

Collaboration tools like Zoom, Slack, and Trello have become the connective tissue of the modern project economy—creating the illusion of proximity even when teams span continents. In this environment, coordination and communication are no longer bound by geography; they are limited only by the quality of digital engagement and shared purpose.

Artificial intelligence (AI) now amplifies this acceleration. AI systems automate what used to be the administrative burden of project management—summarizing meetings, surfacing action items, analyzing risks, and forecasting delivery trends. Advanced generative models interpret complex data sets, create dashboards, and even draft project documentation in near real time. The result is a project ecosystem where human creativity is freed from repetitive tasks, allowing leaders to focus on strategic direction, stakeholder engagement, and innovation.

Perhaps the most transformative enabler of this "acceleration without borders" is **blockchain technology**—the foundation of what Don and Alex Tapscott call "the Internet of Value" in *Blockchain Revolution*. Just as the Internet democratized access to information, blockchain democratizes access to trust and verification. Instead of relying on central authorities or intermediaries to confirm transactions, blockchain enables distributed ledgers that are transparent, immutable, and self-verifying.

In project-based work, this opens entirely new pathways. Smart contracts—self-executing agreements coded on the blockchain—can automatically trigger payments, approve deliverables, or release milestones when predefined conditions are met. This eliminates layers of bureaucracy and builds trust directly into the system architecture. Teams can form "trustless" collaborations where accountability is governed by code, not hierarchy.

The implications extend further when combined with AI. Artificial intelligence can monitor blockchain transactions, detect anomalies, and ensure contractual compliance in real time. Meanwhile, blockchain can secure the provenance of data that AI systems rely on—creating a transparent record of how models are trained and how decisions are made. Together, these technologies create a new digital infrastructure for global collaboration: open, automated, and self-governing.

In essence, technology is not just accelerating project work—it's dissolving traditional borders of organization, geography, and even trust. The emerging landscape of AI-augmented, blockchain-verified collaboration points toward a future where work itself becomes decentralized, fluid, and value-driven. The "project" becomes the atomic unit of economic activity, and technology serves as both the medium and the marketplace for human creativity.

Lee Iacocca once said, "The speed of communication is the speed of business." Today, that speed is near real time. A project team can be formed on a Monday, hold a global kickoff by Tuesday, and begin producing measurable outputs before the week is out. This collapse in coordination cost makes temporary, mission-driven teams not just feasible but advantageous.

ECONOMICS: VOLATILITY FAVORS FLEXIBILITY

Economic volatility rewards organizations that can flex capacity quickly. When demand spikes, project contracts allow companies to scale up without committing to permanent headcount. When markets soften, contracts can be paused or completed without the trauma of mass layoffs. Guy Standing's analysis in *The Precariat* underscores the double-edged nature of this flexibility. For organizations, it is a competitive weapon; for workers, it can be a source of insecurity if they fail to build portable skills and networks.

Stephen Covey's principle of "Begin with the End in Mind" is especially relevant here. For leaders, the end is not simply lower cost but sustainable value. A project-based funding model aligns investment with outcomes and allows for rapid reallocation when priorities change. James Altucher echoes this thinking in *Choose Yourself*, urging individuals to diversify income streams and "own their own runway" so that economic shifts become opportunities rather than threats.

DEMOGRAPHICS: A WORKFORCE THAT DEMANDS MEANING AND MOBILITY

Millennials and Gen Z now make up more than half of the global workforce. Surveys show they prioritize purpose, flexibility, and growth over stability for its own sake. Kory Kogon and Suzette Blakemore note in *Project Management for the Unofficial Project Manager* that these generations are naturally drawn to project work because it offers clear goals, defined timelines, and visible results.

Younger workers are also digital natives who expect to leverage technology to work anywhere, anytime. This expectation dovetails perfectly with project-based models. Rather than waiting for promotions in a rigid hierarchy, they can move from project to project, accumulating skills and building a portfolio of achievements that showcase their capabilities to future employers or clients.

THE INTERSECTION: TECHNOLOGY + ECONOMICS + DEMOGRAPHICS

These forces are not isolated; they are interdependent catalysts. Technology fuels flexible work models, economic volatility demands agility, and a new generation of workers expects a dynamic, project-based landscape.

Peter Drucker, often called the father of modern management, captured this spirit of agency when he said, "The best way to predict the future is to create it." In this new world of work, success favors those who step forward, who innovate, adapt, and lead amid uncertainty.

"Making it happen" is no longer a slogan; it's a professional imperative. The leaders of tomorrow will be those who can navigate and shape the convergence of technology, economics, and demographics.

RISKS AND SAFEGUARDS

The benefits of projectization are real, but so are the risks. Income variability can lead to financial stress. Rapid project turnover can erode institutional knowledge. To mitigate these risks, both individuals and organizations must act deliberately.

For individuals, Stephen Covey's habit of "Sharpen the Saw" offers guidance. Continual upskilling, networking, and maintaining health is not optional. James Altucher recommends becoming an "idea machine," generating new project concepts daily to stay ahead of the market.

For organizations, Kogon and Blakemore advocate for lightweight but meaningful governance. Charters, communication plans, and risk registers are not bureaucratic red tape; they are the guardrails that keep flexible teams aligned with strategic goals.

NASA's Advanced Supercomputing Division (NAS) provides a practical illustration. By introducing a project management office with clear templates and review cadences, NAS has balanced agility with accountability. Projects can be launched quickly, but leaders maintain visibility into risk and resource allocation.

Technology removes barriers, economics rewards agility, and demographics demand purpose. These factors explain why the project-based economy is not a fad but a structural transformation. As Lee Iacocca advised, "In times of great change, you can either lead, follow, or get out of the way." The wise choice today is to lead by embracing projects as the primary vehicle for value creation.

KEY TAKEAWAYS

1. Three Forces Are Reshaping Work

- Technology, economics, and demographics are converging to drive the rise of project-based work.
- These forces reinforce one another, creating a self-accelerating cycle of change that favors agility, speed, and innovation.

2. Technology Enables Real-Time Collaboration

- Cloud platforms, AI tools, and digital collaboration suites have collapsed coordination costs, allowing global teams to form and execute projects in days.
- Speed of communication directly shapes speed of

business, making project work a natural fit for the modern operating environment.

3. Economics Rewards Flexibility

- Project contracts allow organizations to scale capacity up or down quickly in response to volatile markets.
- While this gives companies a competitive edge, it also requires individuals to build portable skills, networks, and financial resilience to navigate uncertainty.

4. Demographics Drive Demand for Meaning and Mobility

- Millennials and Gen Z, now the largest share of the workforce, prioritize purpose, flexibility, and growth over rigid hierarchies.
- Project work aligns with their expectations by offering clear goals, defined timelines, and visible impact.

5. Leadership Requires Shaping the Convergence

- As Peter Drucker said, "The best way to predict the future is to create it."
- Leaders who understand how these forces intersect—and design strategies around them—will set the pace in the project economy.

6. Projectization Brings Opportunity and Risk

- Benefits: speed, agility, adaptability, and access to global talent.

- Risks: income volatility, loss of institutional knowledge, and potential burnout.
- Mitigation: deliberate governance, continuous learning, and psychological safety for teams.

7. Safeguards Matter as Much as Speed

- Lightweight governance structures like charters, communication plans, and risk registers provide alignment without adding bureaucracy.
- For individuals, upskilling, networking, and self-renewal are essential to stay competitive.

8. The Choice Is Clear

- As Jack Welch put it, "Change before you have to."
- Those who lead the shift toward projectization will shape its outcomes. Those who don't will simply react to it.

9. AI accelerates collaboration

- By automating meeting summaries, schedule analysis, and reporting, teams are freed to focus on creativity and decision-making.

10. Blockchain builds digital trust

- Through transparent, decentralized verification and secure recordkeeping across global teams.

11. Smart contracts streamline delivery

- By automating approvals, payments, and milestone releases based on predefined conditions.

12. AI and blockchain together

- Create intelligent, self-governing systems that enhance transparency, efficiency, and data integrity.

13. Technology removes borders

- Enabling distributed teams to collaborate seamlessly across geography, time zones, and organizational boundaries.

2

EVIDENCE OF THE SHIFT

It is one thing to claim that work is becoming more project-based; it is another to show the data and lived realities that support it. Across labor markets, technology sectors, and even government agencies, the evidence is mounting that the project paradigm is not merely a theory but a measurable transformation.

LABOR MARKET SIGNALS

Consider the explosive growth of freelance platforms such as Upwork, Toptal, and Fiverr. Each year, they report record revenues and an expanding global talent pool. According to recent labor analyses, contract and independent work have grown several times faster than traditional full-time employment over the past decade. Guy Standing highlighted this trend in *The Precariat*, warning that the rise of gig and contract work is reshaping the very concept of employment security.

Even traditional industries are adapting. Fortune 500 companies now maintain internal gig marketplaces where employees can bid for short-term projects outside their home departments. This allows companies to mobilize talent dynamically while giving employees the variety and skill-building opportunities they crave. James Altucher would describe this as "choosing yourself" inside an enterprise: finding opportunities that may never appear in a job posting but deliver portfolio-worthy outcomes.

TECHNOLOGY ADOPTION METRICS

Software usage provides another layer of evidence. Project collaboration platforms such as Jira, Asana, Smartsheet, Monday.com, and Trello have experienced double-digit annual growth. These tools are not simply digital whiteboards; they are operating systems for the project economy. They make it easy to launch, track, and close projects with transparency.

Artificial intelligence accelerates this trend. Machine learning models can now predict schedule slippage, detect resource bottlenecks, and even draft risk assessments. Stephen Covey's advice to "Put First Things First" resonates in this environment: technology frees humans from routine tasks so they can focus on high-priority decisions and relationships.

ORGANIZATIONAL CASE STUDIES

NASA's Advanced Supercomputing Division offers a living case study. Transitioning from an operations-centric model to a project-based approach, NAS established a Project Management Office to charter initiatives, standardize communication, and measure outcomes. Early results include shorter cycle times, improved forecast accuracy, and a stronger culture of accountability. Lee Iacocca's turnaround of Chrysler decades earlier follows a similar pattern—clear projects, aggressive milestones, and visible accountability—but today's technology amplifies those tactics.

Other examples abound. Banks use project teams to implement new regulatory requirements. Hospitals form rapid-response teams to deploy telemedicine capabilities. Municipal governments launch cross-departmental projects to modernize infrastructure and deliver smart-city services. The unifying factor is a shift from static job descriptions to dynamic project charters.

CULTURAL EVIDENCE

The language of work itself is changing. Terms like "gig," "sprint," and "deliverable" have entered mainstream conversation. Young professionals increasingly describe their careers not in terms of positions held but in projects completed. Kory Kogon and Suzette Blakemore argue that this shift requires a new mindset: everyone is an unofficial project manager. Whether you are leading a marketing campaign, implementing a software upgrade, or organizing a corporate event, the ability to scope, plan, and communicate is now a core competency.

Altucher encourages individuals to leverage this cultural shift by building a "public trail" of contributions, talks, open-source code, templates, and articles that demonstrate expertise beyond any single employer. This public portfolio becomes your true résumé, signaling capability and adaptability to future clients and collaborators.

IMPLICATIONS AND MEANING

The evidence points to a fundamental realignment. For individuals, this means cultivating portable skills and treating each project as a learning opportunity. Stephen Covey's habit of "Seek First to Understand, Then to Be Understood" is invaluable when moving between diverse teams and industries.

For organizations, the takeaway is clear: embrace internal marketplaces, reward outcomes over activity, and sustain a lightweight yet real governance framework. Peter Drucker once warned, "The greatest danger in times of turbulence is not the turbulence; it is to act with yesterday's logic."

This is more than a call to innovate; it's a call to rethink how work itself is structured. Organizations can no longer rely on rigid hierarchies or static processes; they must cultivate fluid ecosystems that harness data, technology, and talent mobility to deliver value through projects as the primary unit of work.

The organizations that thrive in this new paradigm will be those that intentionally design their operating models to adapt, evolve, and scale. They will not simply weather disruption; they will shape the landscape around it.

The project paradigm is visible in labor statistics, technology adoption curves, and the language of work. The question is no longer whether the shift is happening, but how quickly you and your organization will adapt. In the words of Iacocca, "Even a correct decision is wrong when it is taken too late." The time to embrace the project economy is now.

KEY TAKEAWAYS

1. The Shift to Project-Based Work Is Measurable and Real

- Labor market trends, technology adoption metrics, and organizational behaviors all point to a structural transformation, not a passing trend.
- Projects are increasingly the primary units of value delivery, replacing static job roles as the engine of organizational progress.

2. Labor Markets Reflect the New Reality

- Freelance and contract work are growing faster than traditional full-time employment, signaling a more fluid workforce.
- Internal gig marketplaces are emerging within large enterprises, enabling employees to self-select into projects that match their interests and skills.
- Individuals who adopt a portfolio mindset are better positioned to thrive in this evolving landscape.

3. Technology Is the Operating System of the Project Economy

- Collaboration and project management platforms such as Jira, Asana, and Trello have experienced rapid, sustained adoption, making project work more transparent and scalable.
- Artificial intelligence is further accelerating productivity, freeing people to focus on strategic decisions rather than routine coordination.

4. Organizations Are Rewiring How Work Gets Done

- Case studies across industries show organizations replacing rigid hierarchies with flexible project structures to improve cycle times, increase agility, and enhance accountability.
- Project charters, milestones, and outcome-driven funding models are becoming standard practice in both the private and public sectors.

5. Culture Confirms the Shift

- Language and identity in the workplace are changing: professionals increasingly describe their careers in terms of projects completed rather than positions held.
- Everyone, regardless of title, is expected to develop project management skills to remain relevant in dynamic environments.

6. Implications for Individuals

- Building portable skills, cultivating professional networks, and treating each project as a learning opportunity are essential survival strategies.
- A visible project portfolio, open-source contributions, and case studies have become the modern résumé.

7. Implications for Organizations

- Organizations that embrace internal marketplaces, reward outcomes over activity, and adopt lightweight governance models will outpace those clinging to outdated hierarchies.

- As Peter Drucker warned, "The greatest danger in times of turbulence is not the turbulence; it is to act with yesterday's logic."

8. Timing Is Everything

- The evidence is overwhelming: the project economy is here.
- As Lee Iacocca put it, "Even a correct decision is wrong when it is taken too late." Those who act now will shape the future of work, while those who wait will be forced to catch up.

PART TWO
CORE KNOWLEDGE FOR A PROJECTIZED WORLD

1

FRAMEWORKS
AGILE, WATERFALL, AND HYBRID TAILORING

If the first part of this book makes the case for why work is becoming more project-based, this chapter begins the practical journey of operating in that environment. The good news is that we do not have to start from scratch. Decades of project management experience offer proven frameworks—Agile, Waterfall, and Hybrid—that can be tailored to a wide range of contexts.

NO SILVER BULLET

Henry Ford once said, "Don't find fault, find a remedy." The same applies to project frameworks: there is no perfect methodology, only tools for specific problems. Stephen Covey would call this beginning with the end in mind. Before selecting a framework, leaders must ask: What outcomes are we seeking? What level of uncertainty exists? How critical is compliance? Answering these questions upfront allows you to align the framework with the mission rather than forcing the mission into a framework.

AGILE: EMBRACING CHANGE

Agile emerged from software development but now spans marketing, education, and even government projects. It values individuals and interactions over processes and tools, working solutions over exhaustive documentation, and responding to change over following a plan. Scrum, Kanban, and Lean Startup are popular Agile variants.

Key Agile principles include short iterations, continuous feedback, and the delivery of working increments of value. This approach is particularly well-suited to projects where requirements are evolving or innovation is paramount. James Altucher's "choose yourself" ethos aligns perfectly with Agile's spirit of empowerment: teams are not waiting for permission to act—they self-organize, set priorities, and adapt dynamically to feedback.

As Kory Kogon and Suzette Blakemore emphasize, the "unofficial project manager" thrives in Agile environments because leadership is distributed, not centralized. Anyone on the team can step up to remove blockers, clarify direction, or communicate progress. This model depends on trust, accountability, and shared ownership—qualities that develop progressively as teams mature.

Bruce Tuckman's classic framework on team development—*Forming, Storming, Norming, Performing,* and *Adjourning*—offers a powerful lens for understanding this evolution.

- Forming: In the early stages, team members orient themselves, clarify roles, and build initial trust. Agile ceremonies such as sprint planning and daily stand-ups provide structure and create psychological safety.

- Storming: As the team begins to work, conflicts and differing viewpoints emerge. Agile's emphasis on transparency and feedback enables teams to surface issues early, address them collaboratively, and align around shared goals.
- Norming: Once expectations and working agreements solidify, the team develops rhythms and norms. Decision-making becomes more fluid, and individuals begin to step into leadership roles organically.
- Performing: At this stage, the team operates at high velocity with minimal friction. Members anticipate one another's needs, self-manage effectively, and focus on delivering value rather than just completing tasks. Leadership becomes situational and adaptive, allowing innovation to flourish.
- Adjourning: When a project or initiative concludes, Agile teams reflect through retrospectives, capturing lessons learned to carry forward into future efforts. This final stage reinforces learning and enables a smoother transition into new missions.

Agile's strength lies in recognizing that teams are living systems. They grow, adapt, and evolve. When organizations intentionally support this evolution through lightweight governance, psychological safety, and empowerment, they build high-performing, resilient teams capable of delivering continuous value in uncertain and fast-changing environments.

WATERFALL: THE POWER OF PREDICTABILITY

Not every project benefits from constant iteration. Some, such as infrastructure upgrades, regulatory compliance initiatives, and high-stakes engineering, require meticulous planning and sequential execution. Waterfall provides this structure. It divides work into phases—requirements, design, build, test, and deploy—with formal reviews and sign-offs before moving forward.

Lee Iacocca's turnaround of Chrysler relied on Waterfall-like discipline for manufacturing and supply chain projects. In regulated industries or mission-critical operations like NASA's supercomputing upgrades, the rigor of Waterfall ensures accountability and documentation.

HYBRID: THE BEST OF BOTH WORLDS

Most modern projects blend Agile adaptability with Waterfall predictability. A hybrid approach might use Waterfall for upfront security reviews and budgeting, then adopt Agile sprints for design and development. Stephen Covey's habit of "Synergize" captures the essence of Hybrid: combining strengths to create results greater than the sum of the parts.

TAILORING THE FRAMEWORK

Choosing a framework is not a one-time decision. It requires ongoing tailoring as conditions change. Kory Kogon advises leaders to regularly revisit their project approach, asking, "Does our current method still serve the outcome?" James Altucher might call this making "micro-pivots": small, frequent adjustments that prevent small problems from becoming big failures.

Practical Tailoring Checklist:

- Uncertainty: How stable are requirements?
- Compliance: What regulatory or safety constraints apply?
- Integration Complexity: How many systems or teams must align?
- Stakeholder Cadence: How often do sponsors need updates or demos?
- Delivery Risk: What is the cost of failure or delay?
- Team Maturity: How experienced is the team with Agile or Waterfall?

CASE EXAMPLE: NASA NAS HYBRID PRACTICES

At NASA's Advanced Supercomputing Division, project teams often face conflicting needs. Security and compliance demand Waterfall-like documentation, while cutting-edge research requires Agile experimentation. The PMO adopted a hybrid model: charters and risk registers provide upfront clarity, while sprint reviews and demo days allow for iterative learning. This approach reflects Lee Iacocca's philosophy of pragmatic leadership—"apply yourself, get the facts, then act decisively."

CULTURAL CONSIDERATIONS

Frameworks are only as strong as the culture that supports them. Stephen Covey's habit of "Seek First to Understand" is critical when introducing new methods. Teams must feel heard and see the value in changing their workflow. A leader who imposes Agile or Waterfall without dialogue will encounter resistance and superficial compliance.

Frameworks are not dogmas; they are toolboxes. Agile offers speed and adaptability. Waterfall provides rigor and predictability. Hybrid tailoring combines the two for maximum fit. The effective project manager, official or unofficial, understands each method's strengths, selects the right mix, and adapts as conditions evolve. As Lee Iacocca would remind us, "The ability to concentrate and to use your time well is everything." The right framework ensures that concentration is focused where it matters most.

KEY TAKEAWAYS

1. Frameworks Are Tools, Not Dogmas

- There is no single "best" methodology—only the right tool for the problem at hand.
- Choosing between Agile, Waterfall, or Hybrid approaches should begin with a clear understanding of desired outcomes, uncertainty levels, compliance requirements, and stakeholder expectations.
- As Henry Ford said, "Don't find fault, find a remedy." Framework selection is about fit, not ideology.

2. Agile Excels in Environments of Change

- Agile emphasizes short iterations, feedback loops, and working increments of value.
- It empowers self-organizing teams, supports

continuous learning, and adapts well to evolving
requirements.

- Tuckman's model (Forming–Storming–Norming–
Performing–Adjourning) provides a lens to
understand how Agile teams mature over time.

3. Waterfall Provides Structure and Predictability

- Sequential, phase-based execution is effective where
precision, documentation, and accountability are
paramount.
- Ideal for infrastructure, compliance, or mission-
critical work where deviation carries high risk.
- Its strength lies in clarity of scope and rigor of
control.

4. Hybrid Models Offer Strategic Flexibility

- Most modern organizations blend Agile adaptability
with Waterfall discipline.
- Hybrid approaches enable structured planning
upfront (e.g., risk, security, budgeting) while
allowing iterative design and development.
- This balance enables teams to pivot without losing
control.

5. Tailoring Is an Ongoing Process

- Frameworks should evolve as conditions change
through micro-pivots rather than wholesale
reinvention.
- Leaders should regularly ask: "Does our current
method still serve the outcome?"

- Tailoring depends on uncertainty, integration complexity, compliance, delivery risk, stakeholder cadence, and team maturity.

6. Culture Determines Framework Success

- Frameworks fail when imposed without dialogue.
- A culture of psychological safety, trust, and transparency allows Agile, Waterfall, or Hybrid models to work as intended.
- Stephen Covey's "Seek First to Understand" is critical: people adopt what they help build.

7. Leadership and Focus Matter Most

- Frameworks set direction, but leadership converts plans into results.
- As Jack Welch put it, "Good business leaders create a vision, articulate the vision, passionately own the vision, and relentlessly drive it to completion."
- The proper framework, applied with clarity and discipline, ensures that focus and energy are directed where they matter most.

2

THE CHARTER
VISION, SCOPE, AND ALIGNMENT

If a project is a journey, the charter is the map, compass, and travel manifesto combined. It answers the essential questions of why the project exists, what success looks like, and how the team will travel together. Projects do not fail at the end; they fail at the beginning when purpose and scope are unclear.

WHY A CHARTER MATTERS

Peter Drucker once said, "Plans are only good intentions unless they immediately degenerate into hard work." The project charter embodies that principle. It transforms a broad vision into a concrete agreement that sponsors, team members, and stakeholders can reference throughout the project's life. By capturing intent in writing, the charter becomes both a commitment and a compass, ensuring alignment, accountability, and clarity of purpose from initiation through delivery. Stephen Covey's habit of "Begin with the End in Mind" could have been written specifically for this step.

A well-crafted charter provides:

- **Vision & Problem Statement:** Why this project matters and what needs it addresses.
- **Objectives & Success Criteria:** Measurable outcomes that define completion.
- **Scope Boundaries & Deliverables:** What is included and what is explicitly excluded.
- **Stakeholders & Roles:** Clarity of ownership and accountability.
- **Milestones & Risks:** Key checkpoints and known uncertainties.

BUILDING THE CHARTER COLLABORATIVELY

Kory Kogon and Suzette Blakemore emphasize that charters work best when co-created. In *Project Management for the Unofficial Project Manager*, they advocate bringing sponsors, core team members, and key stakeholders together early to define scope and success criteria. This process creates shared ownership and surfaces assumptions before they harden into problems.

James Altucher would describe this as creating an "idea machine." Every participant contributes insights and potential pitfalls. The goal is not a perfect plan but a shared understanding of purpose and direction.

Practical Steps to Draft a Charter

1. **Frame the Why:** Start with a concise problem statement and vision. Avoid jargon. Inspire action.

2. **Define Success:** Specify measurable outcomes. Lee Iacocca liked to say, "Decisions without numbers are just conversations."
3. **Set Boundaries:** Clarify what is out of scope to prevent scope creep.
4. **Identify Stakeholders:** Map who is impacted, who funds the project, and who holds decision authority.
5. **Outline Milestones:** Provide a high-level timeline with key decision points.
6. **List Risks and Assumptions:** Capture known uncertainties and the assumptions behind them.

NASA NAS Example

At NASA's Advanced Supercomputing Division, every major initiative—from GPU cluster integration to network infrastructure upgrades begins with a standardized charter. This template ensures that objectives, resource requirements, and potential risks are visible to leadership before work begins. The result is fewer mid-project surprises and faster approvals.

Living Document, Not Static Artifact

The charter is not a relic to be filed away. It should be revisited at major milestones, updated with approved changes, and used as the baseline for decisions. Stephen Covey's habit of "Put First Things First" reminds us to align daily actions with the project's most important goals. The charter is the reference point for that alignment.

COMMUNICATING THE CHARTER

A charter only works if it is accessible and understood. Too often, charters are drafted with great care but then tucked away in a shared drive or buried in a dense document that no one revisits after kickoff. In fast-moving environments, this makes the charter little more than a ceremonial artifact, something checked off a list rather than used as a living guide. For a charter to have real power, it must be visible, digestible, and woven into the project's daily rhythm.

This is where simplicity becomes a strength. PMOs that prioritize clarity often distill their charters into one-page summaries paired with visual roadmaps. These aren't just aesthetic choices; they make essential elements—such as purpose, scope, major milestones, roles, and responsibilities— easy to understand at a glance. A good charter doesn't overwhelm; it orients. It ensures that everyone, from the executive sponsor to the newest team member, can answer the fundamental questions: *Why are we doing this? What does success look like? How will we get there?*

Henry Gantt, one of the early architects of modern project management, understood this principle long before Agile ceremonies or digital dashboards existed. He remarked, "The real value of any plan is not merely its creation, but its communication and execution." His insight highlights a timeless truth: a plan hidden from view has no power. It is in communicating the plan clearly and consistently that it becomes a tool capable of shaping outcomes.

Building on this, Kory Kogon and Suzette Blakemore emphasize the importance of embedding the communication plan directly into the charter. By defining when, how, and through what channels stakeholders will receive updates, the charter moves beyond vision-setting to become a practical coordination mechanism. It sets expectations upfront, reducing ambiguity later and reinforcing a culture of openness and accountability.

A well-crafted, visible, and well-communicated charter functions as the north star of the project. It's a shared compass, a single point of truth that everyone can refer to as priorities shift and new challenges emerge. In the modern project economy, where teams form, execute, and disband at speed, this level of clarity isn't just good practice—it's a competitive advantage.

A strong charter clarifies purpose, defines success, and aligns stakeholders before a single dollar is spent or a resource is committed. It transforms intent into a shared understanding outlining the *why, what, when,* and *how* of a project. This clarity is more than good governance; it's a strategic advantage.

In the modern project economy, teams often form, execute, and dissolve rapidly, sometimes within weeks or months. In such a dynamic environment, a well-crafted charter acts as a stabilizing anchor. It ensures that everyone—from sponsors to team members—is aligned on objectives, scope, and success criteria, even as conditions evolve.

Beyond alignment, a strong charter also establishes decision-making boundaries, defines ownership, and sets expectations for value delivery. This creates the conditions for teams to move fast without losing coherence, reducing the risk of scope drift, miscommunication, or competing priorities.

Moreover, when projects are launched within a portfolio of strategic initiatives, clear charters enable leaders to prioritize intelligently, allocate resources efficiently, and measure progress objectively. In other words, the charter becomes the currency of clarity in a projectized world, enabling speed and adaptability without sacrificing accountability.

KEY TAKEAWAYS

1. The Charter Is the Foundation of Every Project

- A strong charter clarifies why a project exists, what success looks like, and how and when the team will achieve it.
- Most project failures begin at the start; unclear purpose and scope are the root cause.
- As Peter Drucker said, "Plans are only good intentions unless they immediately degenerate into hard work." The charter turns intentions into actionable direction.

2. Clarity Drives Alignment

- A well-structured charter includes vision, scope boundaries, success criteria, stakeholders, milestones, and risks.
- It provides a single point of truth for sponsors, team members, and stakeholders, ensuring shared understanding and accountability.
- Stephen Covey's principle "Begin with the End in Mind" is embodied in this step.

3. Co-Creation Builds Ownership

- Charters are most effective when built collaboratively rather than handed down.
- Early involvement of sponsors, team members, and key stakeholders surfaces assumptions, builds trust, and fosters commitment.
- Collaboration transforms the charter from a document into a shared agreement.

4. Communication Makes the Charter Real

- A charter loses value if it's hidden in a shared drive or buried in dense documentation.
- Simplifying the charter into one-page summaries and visual roadmaps keeps it visible, accessible, and actionable.
- Henry Gantt's insight remains timeless: "The real value of any plan is not merely its creation, but its communication and execution."

5. The Charter Must Live, Not Sit on a Shelf

- Effective teams revisit and update the charter at key milestones as conditions evolve.
- Embedding the communication plan directly into the charter sets clear expectations for updates and decision-making.
- This transforms the charter from a launch artifact into an ongoing alignment mechanism.

6. Strategic Advantage Through Clarity

- In fast-moving environments where teams form and dissolve quickly, the charter acts as a stabilizing anchor.
- Clear charters prevent scope drift, reduce miscommunication, and enable teams to move fast without losing coherence.
- At the portfolio level, strong charters support intelligent prioritization, resource allocation, and objective progress tracking.

7. Leadership Starts with Vision

- A charter is both a leadership tool and a governance instrument.
- When leaders invest in clarity upfront, they minimize confusion downstream.
- In the project economy, the charter is not just documentation—it is the currency of clarity that enables both speed and accountability.

3
COMMUNICATION AS THE OPERATING SYSTEM

Projects run on communication. Scope, schedule, risk, and cost may form the structural framework, but it is communication that keeps the engine running. When communication fails, even the best plans collapse. In a project economy defined by cross-functional teams, distributed workforces, and rapid change, communication is not a side activity; it is the operating system of success. San Francisco 49ers Super Bowl-winning coach Bill Walsh believed "that success begins with standards, especially communication standards." He demanded precision not only in how plays were executed but in how they were discussed, briefed, and reviewed. His philosophy applies directly to modern projects: when leaders establish clear communication rhythms and expectations, execution improves not because they push harder, but because the team already knows the language of winning.

WHY COMMUNICATION MATTERS

Stephen Covey's timeless habit, "Seek First to Understand, Then to Be Understood," captures the very heart of effective project communication. Before persuading, influencing, or mobilizing others, project leaders must listen deeply. This means going beyond surface-level updates and status reports to uncover hidden concerns, unspoken constraints, and competing priorities that shape the real dynamics of a project. It's through this empathetic listening that trust is built, alignment is achieved, and resistance can be transformed into commitment.

Peter Drucker, the father of modern management, once remarked, "The most important thing in communication is hearing what isn't said." His words speak to a profound truth: communication is not just about transmitting information. It's about perceiving nuance, identifying gaps, and understanding the human dimension of projects. Great project leaders don't just speak well; they listen well, sensing risks and tensions long before they surface. Bill Walsh emphasized that "how a leader communicates under pressure sets the emotional tone for the entire team." When situations intensified on the field, his voice grew calmer. His clarity and steadiness created confidence and alignment. In projects, moments of uncertainty are inevitable; leaders who communicate with Walsh's discipline turn potential chaos into coordinated action.

Henry Gantt, a pioneer of modern project planning, understood the central role of communication in execution. He noted, "A man doing his best always becomes better." This simple yet powerful idea reflects that when people are well informed, clearly directed, and meaningfully engaged, they are capable of improving not only their work but the team's collective performance. Clear communication fuels that improvement. It allows individuals to contribute with confidence, collaborate with intention, and continuously raise the bar.

Lee Iacocca echoed this sentiment from a leadership perspective when he said, "You can have brilliant ideas, but if you can't get them across, your ideas won't get you anywhere." In today's project economy, communication is more than a courtesy—it's a strategic enabler. It connects vision to execution, aligns diverse stakeholders, accelerates decision-making, and turns good ideas into tangible outcomes.

In a world where teams are fluid, fast-moving, and distributed, communication is what binds everything together. It ensures that strategy does not live only in leadership decks, that risks are not buried in silence, and that every contributor sees how their efforts connect to a larger purpose.

Simply put, communication isn't an accessory to project management; it is the operating system of effective delivery.

Elements of a Communication Plan

A robust communication plan defines audiences, messages, cadences, and channels. Kory Kogon and Suzette Blakemore advise creating a one-page plan linked directly to the project charter.

This plan should answer:

- Who needs to know what?
- How often?
- Through which channels (email, meetings, dashboards, instant messaging)?

- What decisions or actions are expected after each communication?

The plan must also specify feedback mechanisms. Communication is not a broadcast; it is a dialogue. NASA's NAS PMO meetings, for example, always include open Q&A segments to surface risks and dependencies.

MAKING STATUS USEFUL

Project updates often fail because they focus on activity rather than progress. Useful status reports highlight:

- Deltas: What has changed since the last update?
- Risks and blockers: Issues that threaten schedule or quality.
- Decisions needed: Specific actions required from sponsors or stakeholders.

James Altucher encourages individuals to "over-communicate clarity." In a world of information overload, brevity and relevance are acts of respect. Visual dashboards, one-page reports, and concise email summaries help stakeholders grasp the essentials quickly.

BUILDING TRUST THROUGH TRANSPARENCY

Projects thrive when team members feel safe to raise issues early. Transparency builds trust, and trust accelerates delivery. Covey's concept of the "emotional bank account" is a helpful metaphor: every act of clear, honest communication is a deposit; every missed update or hidden risk is a withdrawal. Maintain a positive balance by sharing bad news early and framing it with options for resolution. Bill Walsh famously said, "Champions behave like champions before they're champions." He modeled transparency and accountability himself, holding every communication, especially bad news, to the highest standard. When leaders consistently communicate with honesty and precision, they don't just inform teams; they set the cultural standard everyone rises to meet.

TECHNOLOGY AS A COMMUNICATION MULTIPLIER

Modern collaboration tools make communication instantaneous, but they also create noise. Leaders must balance real-time channels like Slack with asynchronous updates such as weekly summaries. Bill Walsh would have called this setting the "standard of clarity." He believed every message must serve a purpose: to align, direct, or inspire. In an era of constant pings and chatter, disciplined communication isn't just efficient; it's a leadership act. Lee Iacocca warned against mistaking activity for progress. Choose the fewest channels that reach the widest audience with the highest clarity.

NASA Case Example

At NASA's Advanced Supercomputing Division, weekly dependency stand-ups and monthly portfolio reviews ensure that critical information flows across teams. The PMO uses a standardized one-page status template focusing on changes, blockers, and required decisions. This keeps leadership informed without overwhelming them with detail.

Practical Tips

- Begin every meeting by stating the decision or outcome sought.
- Use visuals to explain complex dependencies.
- Encourage dissent and debate before decisions; practice "disagree and commit" afterward.
- Document key actions and owners within 24 hours of each meeting.

Communication is the invisible infrastructure of project success. Plans and schedules are worthless if stakeholders are misaligned or uninformed. As Lee Iacocca observed, "The ability to get along with people is as important as being technically competent."

Bill Walsh's leadership philosophy reminds us that when communication standards are high, execution becomes inevitable. When leaders build cultures of clarity and trust, projects align, decisions accelerate, and results follow. As he proved on the field, "The score takes care of itself." In a project economy where teams form and dissolve rapidly, mastering the art of communication is not optional; it is the core competency that drives every other metric.

KEY TAKEAWAYS

1. Communication Is the True Operating System of Projects

- Scope, schedule, and cost set the structure, but communication keeps everything moving.
- When communication breaks down, even the best plans fail.

- In a project-based, cross-functional, distributed team economy, communication isn't supplemental—it's foundational.

2. Listening Is as Important as Speaking

- Stephen Covey's "Seek First to Understand, Then to Be Understood" underscores the power of empathetic listening.
- Peter Drucker's reminder—"The most important thing in communication is hearing what isn't said"—highlights the need to detect subtle risks, tensions, and gaps before they surface.
- Great project leaders build trust through **listening first**, then communicating with clarity.

3. Clarity Converts Ideas Into Action

- As Lee Iacocca put it, "You can have brilliant ideas, but if you can't get them across, your ideas won't get you anywhere."
- Communication connects vision to execution, accelerates decision-making, and turns plans into outcomes.
- Clear, concise, and relevant messages earn attention and build alignment.

4. A Good Communication Plan Is Structured and Simple

- Define **who** needs to know **what, when**, and **how**.
- Link the communication plan directly to the project charter for consistency.

- Include feedback loops—communication is a dialogue, not a broadcast.

5. Focus on Progress, Not Activity

- Effective status updates emphasize what changed, what's at risk, and what decisions are needed.
- Brevity and relevance cut through noise and respect stakeholders' time.
- Visual dashboards and one-page summaries increase clarity and retention.

6. Transparency Builds Trust and Speed

- Early, honest communication about risks builds credibility and accelerates delivery.
- Every update is either a deposit or a withdrawal from the team's **"emotional bank account."**
- Transparency enables teams to solve problems before they escalate.

7. Technology Is a Tool, Not a Substitute for Leadership

- Collaboration platforms amplify communication but can also create **noise**.
- Leaders must set norms, balance real-time vs. asynchronous communication, and prioritize clarity over volume.
- The right channel at the right time beats more channels all the time.

8. Communication Is Leadership in Action

- Leaders communicate to align, empower, and mobilize — not just to inform.
- As Lee Iacocca said, *"The ability to get along with people is as important as being technically competent."*
- In the project economy, mastering communication is the single most transferable leadership skill.

PART THREE
CASEWORK FROM NASA'S ADVANCED SUPERCOMPUTING (NAS)

1

PROJECT CONTEXT
NAS AND THE PMO MANDATE

The NASA Advanced Supercomputing (NAS) Division at Ames Research Center provides one of the world's most powerful computing environments for science and engineering. From weather modeling to space exploration, NAS supports research that demands extraordinary computational resources and precision.

Historically, NAS operated under a service-centric model in which tasks were assigned and executed as ongoing operations. While effective for stable workloads, this approach limited flexibility when priorities shifted or when projects required cross-disciplinary collaboration. The High-End Computing Capability (HECC) program faced growing demands for speed, transparency, and resource optimization. Leadership recognized the need for a Project Management Office (PMO) to introduce a more structured, project-based model.

Why Projectization Was Necessary

- **Increasing Complexity:** Projects such as GPU cluster integrations, secure enclave configurations, and data center upgrades require coordination across multiple engineering and security teams.
- **Stakeholder Visibility:** Sponsors and NASA leadership needed real-time insight into progress, risks, and resource allocation.
- **Resource Alignment:** Budget constraints and evolving research priorities required flexible but accountable allocation of computing resources.

THE PMO MANDATE

The newly established PMO set out to deliver three core outcomes:

- **Standardization:** Introduce charters, communication plans, and risk registers to create a consistent baseline for all projects.
- **Transparency:** Provide portfolio dashboards and weekly status updates to give leadership clear visibility.
- **Governance:** Implement a lightweight change-control process to manage dependencies and scope adjustments without unnecessary bureaucracy.

BUSINESS-FRIENDLY PRACTICES

Rather than imposing heavy processes, the PMO adopted a pragmatic approach. Charters were designed to fit on a single page. Weekly dependency stand-ups replaced long status meetings. Hybrid–Agile–Waterfall frameworks allowed teams to meet strict security requirements while maintaining iterative development cycles.

LEADERSHIP LESSONS

Stephen Covey's principle of "Put First Things First" guided the PMO's prioritization. By focusing on high-value projects and clarifying decision rights, the team avoided spreading resources too thin. Regular cross-team reviews fostered trust and ensured that issues were identified and addressed early.

Results and Early Wins

Within the first year, NAS reported measurable improvements:

- Reduced project cycle times through clearer charters and milestones.
- Higher forecast accuracy by tracking variance across projects.
- Improved stakeholder satisfaction through transparent dashboards and timely status reports.

Key Takeaways for Other Organizations

The NAS experience shows that even highly technical, mission-critical environments benefit from projectization when it is implemented with a business-friendly mindset. Clear charters, consistent communication, and lightweight governance provide the structure needed for accountability without stifling innovation.

The PMO at NASA NAS demonstrates that project-based management is not just for private industry. When done thoughtfully, it strengthens mission delivery, supports innovation, and provides the visibility leaders need to make confident decisions in a rapidly changing environment.

KEY TAKEAWAYS

1. Even Highly Technical Environments Benefit from Projectization

- Moving from a service-centric to a project-based operating model gave NAS greater flexibility, visibility, and accountability.
- Structured project management is not exclusive to private industry—it is equally valuable in mission-driven, technical, and government settings.

2. Projectization Was a Strategic Response to Complexity

- Modern HPC initiatives—such as GPU cluster integrations, secure enclaves, and infrastructure upgrades—require tight coordination across engineering, security, and operations teams.
- A PMO framework enabled leadership to manage increasing project complexity without losing operational reliability.

3. Visibility and Resource Alignment Are Critical

- Sponsors and stakeholders require real-time insight into progress, risks, and resource allocation.
- Transparent dashboards and weekly updates provided leadership with confidence to prioritize intelligently and allocate resources where they mattered most.

4. PMO Structures Should Be Lightweight, Not Burdensome

- Success came from pragmatic, business-friendly practices, not heavy bureaucracy.
  - One-page charters replaced lengthy templates.
  - Weekly stand-ups replaced sprawling status meetings.
  - Hybrid frameworks balanced security rigor with agility.
- The emphasis was on clarity, speed, and accountability.

5. Leadership Focus Was on Value, Not Volume

- Applying Stephen Covey's "Put First Things First" helped leadership focus on high-impact projects rather than trying to do everything at once.
- Regular cross-team reviews built **trust and alignment**, enabling proactive issue resolution rather than reactive firefighting.

6. Measurable Results Validated the Shift

- Reduced project cycle times through clear scoping and milestone tracking.
- Increased forecast accuracy by systematically monitoring variance.
- Improved stakeholder satisfaction through **transparent and timely communication**.

7. The Right PMO Model Accelerates Mission Delivery

- When projectization is introduced with a clear mandate and adaptive governance, it enables both innovation and control.
- Lightweight PMO practices enhance mission performance while maintaining agility in dynamic environments.

8. Lessons for Other Organizations

- Clarity beats complexity—start with simple, standardized tools and scale as needed.
- Communication is the operating system of projectized work—build visibility into the process from day one.
- Projectization done right doesn't slow teams down—it frees them to move faster with confidence.

2

RATIONALE, SCOPE, AND GOVERNANCE

Once the NASA NAS Project Management Office (PMO) was established, the next critical step was to define why the new model existed, what it would and would not cover, and how decisions would be made. Clarity on these three fronts rationale, scope, and governance—turned an abstract concept into an operational reality.

THE RATIONALE: WHY PROJECTIZATION WAS ESSENTIAL

NAS leaders faced an environment of accelerating demand for computing resources, strict cybersecurity mandates, and growing complexity in research partnerships. Operational workflows that once sufficed for routine upgrades could no longer keep pace. The PMO's creation was not a paperwork exercise; it was a strategic response to three pressing needs:

- Visibility for Leadership: NASA sponsors and federal oversight bodies required real-time insight into project status and risk exposure.

- Predictable Delivery: Scientists and mission managers needed confidence that computing capacity would be ready when scheduled launches or experiments required it.
- Efficient Resource Allocation: Budget cycles required aligning scarce engineering talent with the highest-value initiatives.

DEFINING THE SCOPE

The PMO charter set clear boundaries to avoid scope creep during its formative phase:

- In Scope: All infrastructure upgrades, hardware refreshes, network changes, and major software integrations within the NAS facility.
- Out of Scope (for now): Enterprise-wide policy changes, mission science deliverables outside NAS, and wholesale tooling overhauls.

This focus allowed the PMO to demonstrate quick wins without overextending its authority. As Lee Iacocca advised, "Start with small victories. They build momentum and credibility."

GOVERNANCE FRAMEWORK

With rationale and scope established, the PMO turned to governance—the set of decision rights, escalation paths, and oversight mechanisms that would guide projects from initiation to closeout. The challenge was to provide structure without slowing innovation.

Key Governance Elements:

- Project Charter Approval: All projects require a one-page charter reviewed by the PMO lead and technical sponsor.
- Change Control Board (CCB): A lightweight board meets biweekly to assess scope changes, significant risks, or resource reallocations. Decisions are logged in a shared register for transparency.
- Dependency Stand-Ups: Weekly 15-minute sessions identify cross-project risks and synchronize schedules.
- Quarterly Portfolio Review: Leadership reviews progress, reprioritizes projects, and reallocates resources as needed.

Decision Flow Example

Suppose a GPU cluster upgrade requires an unplanned network reconfiguration. The project manager submits a change request via a simple online form. The PMO lead screens the request and forwards it to the CCB. Within days, the board evaluates the technical impact, budget implications, and scheduling risks. If approved, the change is logged and communicated to all affected teams. This process provides speed and accountability, critical in a high-stakes environment.

LEADERSHIP AND CULTURE

Stephen Covey's habit of "Think Win-Win" influenced the governance design. Rather than framing oversight as control, the PMO presented governance as a shared safety net that protects teams from last-minute surprises. Kory Kogon and Suzette Blakemore emphasize that effective governance should empower teams rather than burden them. By maintaining short meetings, clear templates, and fast decision cycles, the PMO avoided the bureaucracy trap.

Early Outcomes

- Within months, the governance model produced measurable benefits:
- Fewer mid-project delays thanks to proactive dependency reviews.
- Improved sponsor confidence through transparent change tracking.
- Higher team satisfaction because decisions were made quickly and documented clearly.

LESSONS FOR OTHER ORGANIZATIONS

The NAS experience shows that governance is not about control—it is about clarity. By defining decision rights and escalation paths, organizations can move faster and reduce risk. James Altucher's advice to "create your own runway" applies here: build internal processes before external forces demand them.

Rationale provides the why, scope sets the boundaries, and governance creates the rules of the game. Together, they transform a PMO from a concept into a value-delivering engine. As Lee Iacocca reminded his teams, "The ability to concentrate and to use your time well is everything." Governance is the discipline that keeps that concentration focused on what matters most.

KEY TAKEAWAYS

1. Rationale, Scope, and Governance Turn Vision Into Action

- A PMO is only effective when its purpose, boundaries, and decision-making processes are clearly defined.
- These three elements transform projectization from an abstract concept into an operational system that delivers value.

2. Rationale Anchors the "Why"

- NAS faced increasing demand, cybersecurity mandates, and operational complexity that outgrew traditional workflows.
- The PMO was created as a strategic response to these pressures—to provide leadership visibility, predictable delivery, and efficient resource allocation.
- A clear rationale aligns stakeholders around shared priorities and reduces resistance to change.

3. Scope Provides Strategic Focus

- Defining what is in scope and what is out of scope prevented early overreach and allowed the PMO to deliver quick, credible wins.
- Lee Iacocca's reminder to "Start with small victories. They build momentum and credibility" reflects the power of focused implementation.
- Clear scope boundaries prevent mission creep and keep teams aligned on achievable objectives.

4. Governance Enables Speed and Accountability

- Effective governance is **lightweight, structured, and transparent**—not bureaucratic.
- NAS's governance model included:
  - One-page project charters for quick approval.
  - A biweekly Change Control Board (CCB) for structured decisions.
  - Weekly dependency stand-ups for risk mitigation.
  - Quarterly portfolio reviews for strategic realignment.
- These mechanisms accelerated decisions while maintaining oversight.

5. Governance Is a Safety Net, Not a Straitjacket

- By framing governance as a shared protection against last-minute surprises, rather than top-down control, leadership fostered trust.
- Covey's "Think Win-Win" principle informed the model, ensuring governance empowered rather than constrained teams.
- Fast decision cycles, short meetings, and simple templates kept processes lean and respected team autonomy.

6. Early Results Validate the Model

- Reduced mid-project delays through proactive dependency management.
- Greater sponsor confidence thanks to transparent change tracking.

- Higher team satisfaction due to clarity, speed, and documented decisions.

7. Governance Is a Strategic Asset

- Clear decision rights and escalation paths make organizations more agile, not less.
- James Altucher's idea of "creating your own runway" applies: build internal governance discipline before external pressures force it.
- Governance allows leaders to concentrate resources and attention on what matters most.

8. Lessons for Other Organizations

- Start small, define scope tightly, and build credibility with early wins.
- Keep governance visible, fast, and lightweight to avoid bureaucracy.
- Treat governance as an **enabler of speed, alignment, and risk reduction**, not as an obstacle.

3
METHODS, MEASURES, AND FINDINGS

A Project Management Office is only as credible as the evidence it produces. After defining rationale, scope, and governance, the NASA NAS PMO turned to the question of measurement. How do we know if projectization is working? How do we track both hard metrics and the softer signals of cultural change?

METHODS

The PMO adopted a mixed-method approach combining quantitative data analysis with qualitative feedback.

Quantitative Methods:

- Cycle Time Analysis: Comparing planned vs. actual completion dates across projects to measure schedule efficiency.
- Forecast Accuracy: Tracking variance between baseline and current forecasts to identify patterns of over- or under-estimation.

- Resource Utilization: Monitoring engineering hours and hardware allocations to optimize workload distribution.
- Risk Closure Rate: Measuring the percentage of identified risks mitigated within planned timeframes.

Qualitative Methods

- Stakeholder Interviews: Gathering insights from scientists, engineers, and sponsors on communication quality and decision speed.
- Team Retrospectives: Conducting quarterly sessions to capture lessons learned and surface cultural issues.
- Observation of Rituals: Evaluating the effectiveness of stand-ups, portfolio reviews, and change board meetings in promoting transparency and engagement.

MEASURES

Drawing on Stephen Covey's "Put First Things First," the PMO focused on a concise set of measures that directly link to mission outcomes. Instead of overwhelming dashboards with dozens of metrics, the team concentrated on five key indicators:

- Throughput: Number of projects completed per quarter.
- Forecast Accuracy: Percentage of projects finishing within 10% of their planned schedule.
- Dependency Risk Index: Weighted score of unresolved cross-project dependencies.
- Stakeholder Satisfaction: Ratings collected through Lessons Learned documentation.

- Process Adoption Rate: Percentage of projects using standardized charters, risk registers, and communication plans.

Findings

The first year of data yielded several important insights:

- Projects with clearly defined charters achieved a 25% higher forecast accuracy than those launched with minimal documentation.
- Teams that held weekly dependency stand-ups reported fewer mid-project delays.
- Stakeholder satisfaction improved when one-page status reports replaced lengthy email chains.
- Qualitative interviews revealed a **slow** cultural shift among engineers who reported a slight increase in confidence in leadership decisions and clearer priorities.

CULTURAL RESISTANCE TO CHANGE

Change within an organization is rarely just a technical problem—it is, at its core, a human one. Even the most well-designed processes, clean metrics, or elegant workflows can falter when people do not feel seen, heard, or respected in the process of transformation.

In this case, the PMO's introduction of new project governance structures and tools looked strong on paper. The dashboards were clear, the reporting cadence was defined, and the governance framework was meticulously documented. However, the staff's lived experience was very different. What began as a process improvement initiative quickly revealed a cultural gap: a misalignment between how leadership envisioned change and how the workforce experienced it.

A Top-Down Rollout

The implementation was heavily top-down. Leadership dictated the new operating model, selected the tools, and defined the workflows. There was little room for meaningful input from engineers, analysts, and coordinators who relied on these systems every day. While this approach initially created friction, it ultimately opened the door for staff insights to shape refinements that leadership came to appreciate and embrace.

As one engineer recalled, "We weren't asked for our perspective—we were told what was going to happen."

This sentiment was echoed repeatedly in interviews. Employees described the rollout as directive, not collaborative, a textbook example of "do as I say" management. Even those who didn't openly resist found themselves quietly disengaged, following the new process out of obligation rather than commitment. It was a cultural disaster that led to heavy turnover.

Peter Drucker once wrote, "The most important thing in communication is hearing what isn't said."

That insight proved painfully relevant here. Leadership focused on what they wanted to communicate, but they failed to listen to what the staff wasn't saying: the frustration, the skepticism, and the sense that their expertise was being overlooked. When those signals go unacknowledged, even the best-intentioned initiatives risk losing credibility before they begin.

Friction at the Front Line

When communication flows in only one direction, even well-intentioned changes can create unintended resistance. Staff quickly grew frustrated with excessive documentation requirements, unreliable project management tools, and the perception that leadership prioritized compliance over collaboration. What might have been seen as efficiency improvements instead became symbols of control, demeaning management tactics, and a toxic environment.

In team discussions and informal conversations, employees expressed feeling unheard, with their day-to-day realities being ignored in favor of high-level reporting. This gap between policy and practice widened as early hiccups were met not with dialogue, but with more enforcement and threats.

The result: compliance without conviction. The work was getting done, but the energy, trust, and sense of shared purpose that underpin high-performing teams were absent.

The Turning Point

Over time, as routines became familiar and communication channels opened, some teams began to see practical value in the new framework.

One engineer captured this shift well, saying, "The templates felt like extra work at first, but now they save time because everyone knows where to find the latest information."

This is a critical inflection point in any organizational change effort. Discipline often feels like friction before it feels like efficiency. What changed here wasn't the tool itself but how leadership engaged the people who used it. If the staff's voices had been acknowledged and their feedback incorporated, resistance would have dissolved, and adoption would have been more organic.

Lightweight Governance vs. Heavy-Handed Control

Kory Kogon and Suzette Blakemore emphasize that lightweight governance, when consistently applied, ultimately saves time rather than consumes it. However, achieving this outcome requires trust and co-creation. Early on, the PMO made the classic mistake of focusing on *the system's structure* while neglecting *the psychology of the people* who would use it.

Governance should provide guardrails, not handcuffs. When done well, it empowers teams to move quickly with confidence rather than slow down under the weight of compliance. But this can only happen when those affected by the change feel ownership in how it's designed and implemented.

Henry Gantt, whose methods helped shape modern project management, captured this spirit succinctly: "Efficiency must be based on cooperation, not coercion."

The PMO's early efforts leaned too heavily on control. It is only when cooperation replaces compliance that communication becomes a two-way dialogue, and the new processes begin to function as intended.

LESSONS FOR THE FUTURE

The most enduring lesson of this experience is clear: top-down change can enforce compliance, but only collaborative change builds commitment.

Future PMO initiatives would need to be structured differently:

- Early involvement of end users, particularly engineers and operational staff, in tool and process design.
- Two-way communication loops, ensuring feedback doesn't just travel upward but also returns in the form of visible adjustments.
- Transparent rationale for change, helping staff understand *why* processes are shifting—not just *what* is changing.
- Empowerment over enforcement, cultivating a culture where employees feel they have a voice in shaping their own workflows.

In the project economy, where teams form, execute, and disband at unprecedented speed, culture is not a soft factor; it is a strategic lever. A process may be efficient, but without shared ownership, it will never be embraced.

Leaders who recognize this move from command-and-control to co-creation and shared accountability. When that shift happens, what was once seen as "management's process" becomes "our process." That is the moment when change stops being resisted and starts being lived.

LEADERSHIP INSIGHTS

Lee Iacocca believed that "management is nothing more than motivating other people." Data provides the credibility, but leadership provides the motivation. PMO leaders used the metrics not as punitive tools but as conversation starters to celebrate wins and address systemic issues.

Lessons for Other Organizations

James Altucher advises building an "idea machine" and experimenting with small, measurable changes. The NAS PMO followed this principle by treating each metric as a hypothesis. For example, would adding a dependency stand-up reduce schedule variance? The data confirmed it, leading to wider adoption.

By combining quantitative metrics with qualitative feedback, the NAS PMO built a balanced view of progress. The result was not only improved delivery predictability but also a cultural transformation toward transparency and continuous improvement. As Stephen Covey would say, measurement sharpened the saw, turning abstract goals into actionable habits that drive mission success.

KEY TAKEAWAYS

1. Credibility Comes from Evidence, Not Intention

- A PMO's effectiveness is measured not by its existence, but by the evidence it produces.
- By combining quantitative metrics (cycle times, forecast accuracy, utilization) with qualitative insights (interviews, retrospectives), the NAS PMO built a credible, balanced view of impact.
- Data became a **strategic lever**, not just a reporting requirement.

2. Fewer, Meaningful Metrics Drive Focus

- Instead of overwhelming dashboards, the PMO concentrated on five key measures:

- o Throughput
- o Forecast Accuracy
- o Dependency Risk Index
- o Stakeholder Satisfaction
- o Process Adoption Rate
- This focus linked measurement directly to mission outcomes and decision-making.
- Stephen Covey's "Put First Things First" is reflected here: **measure what matters**.

3. Data Validated the Power of Good Practices

- Projects with clear charters had 25% better forecast accuracy.
- Weekly dependency stand-ups reduced mid-project delays.
- One-page status reports improved stakeholder satisfaction.
- These measurable outcomes demonstrated that simple practices applied consistently can yield significant performance gains.

4. Cultural Resistance Was as Real as the Metrics

- Even the best-designed governance and tools falter if people feel unheard or overruled.
- The PMO's top-down rollout created early resistance: staff felt dictated to, not included.
- As Peter Drucker said, "The most important thing in communication is hearing what isn't said."
  Leadership initially missed those unspoken signals.

5. Compliance Without Conviction Is Not Success

- Friction at the front lines emerged from over-documentation, unreliable tools, and one-way communication.
- Early adoption was driven by obligation rather than commitment—work was completed, but trust was lacking.
- This gap highlighted the difference between enforcing compliance and cultivating shared ownership.

6. Turning Point: From Control to Cooperation

- Over time, once feedback loops opened and staff saw their voices reflected in adjustments, adoption became more organic.
- What initially felt like overhead turned into efficiency: "The templates felt like extra work at first, but now they save time."
- Henry Gantt's timeless principle applies: "Efficiency must be based on cooperation, not coercion."

7. Governance Must Be Lightweight and Human-Centered

- Tools and processes must **enable**, not control.
- Real success came when governance provided guardrails, not handcuffs, and when engineers and staff had a real seat at the table.
- Kory Kogon and Suzette Blakemore's emphasis on co-creation proved essential for cultural buy-in.

8. Leadership Turns Data Into Motivation

- Metrics are not punitive tools—they're conversation starters.
- As Lee Iacocca said, "Management is nothing more than motivating other people."
- Leaders used measurements to celebrate wins, surface systemic issues, and build trust, not fear.

9. Lessons for Other Organizations

- Co-create processes rather than imposing them top-down.
- Build two-way communication loops, where feedback drives real adjustments.
- Explain the *why*, not just the *what*, behind new systems.
- Start small—as James Altucher advises, experiment with "idea machine" thinking and scale what works.

10. Measurement Sharpens the Saw

- Metrics provide clarity, but cultural listening offers staying power.
- When both are integrated, PMOs can accelerate delivery, increase predictability, and foster a culture of trust and continuous improvement.
- In Covey's terms, measurement transformed abstract goals into habits that drive mission success.

4

ETHICS, CONSENT, AND DIGNITY IN ORGANIZATIONAL CHANGE

Projectization is not merely a structural shift; it is a profoundly human experience. Behind every charter, schedule, and risk register are people whose careers, identities, and well-being are directly affected by the decisions leaders make. When an organization transitions to a formal Project Management Office (PMO), its success depends as much on ethical engagement as on technical execution.

THE ETHICAL IMPERATIVE

Organizational change can unsettle even the most seasoned teams. Roles are redefined, reporting lines shift, and long-standing routines are disrupted. For leaders, "something positive" must include more than operational outcomes; it must encompass safeguarding dignity, respecting individual agency, and ensuring that change is not only efficient but fair.

Core Ethical Principles

To navigate this transition responsibly, many organizations adopt principles that guide behavior, decisions, and communication throughout the change process. Four of the most critical are:

- Informed Consent: Staff are briefed on what projectization means for their roles and invited to provide feedback before processes are finalized.
- Transparency: Decisions regarding governance, metrics, and resource allocation are communicated openly, with documentation accessible to all stakeholders.
- Respect for Autonomy: Teams are encouraged to propose their own micro-pivots and process improvements that make the new system work better for them.
- Equity: Opportunities to lead initiatives or present at portfolio reviews are distributed broadly to avoid favoritism and ensure balanced representation.

Practical Applications

To uphold these principles, PMOs can implement mechanisms such as:

- Open Forums: Regular Q&A sessions where staff can raise concerns directly with leadership.
- Feedback Loops: Anonymous surveys and structured conversations to gauge perceptions of workload balance, clarity of roles, and communication quality.
- Consent in Data Use: Clear communication on how performance data is collected, stored, and shared,

ensuring individuals understand and agree to how information is used.

These practices echo Stephen Covey's habit, "Seek First to Understand, Then to Be Understood," ensuring that leadership decisions are grounded in listening rather than assumption.

BALANCING SPEED WITH HUMANITY

One of the most common challenges during large-scale change is balancing the need for speed with the need for psychological safety. Rapid project launches can unintentionally leave some employees feeling excluded or pressured. To address this, some organizations include a short section in each project charter focused on stakeholder impact, requiring acknowledgment or sign-off from affected team leads. This ensures that changes are not only technically approved but socially acknowledged, creating space for both urgency and dignity.

QUALITATIVE INSIGHTS

Interviews may reveal that staff deeply value the PMO's openness and transparency, even when decisions are difficult or unpopular. While not everyone agrees with every strategic or operational choice, employees consistently express that being informed and included in the conversation matters just as much as the outcomes themselves.

One engineer puts it this way: "I don't have to agree with every decision, but I do need to understand how it was made."

This simple statement reflects a powerful cultural reality. When people can see the reasoning behind a decision, the trade-offs, priorities, and constraints, they are far more willing to engage constructively and support the direction, even if it doesn't fully align with their personal preferences.

This trust does not appear overnight. It is earned through consistent communication, transparent documentation, and a leadership posture that explains its reasoning rather than issuing directives from the top down. As employees see their feedback acknowledged, even when it is not fully adopted, they begin to place confidence in the process, not just in personalities or positions of authority.

This trust becomes a critical enabler of faster project cycles. Teams are more willing to adapt to shifting priorities, accept necessary trade-offs, and support rapid launches because they understand the *why* behind the *what*. What might once have felt like imposed decisions evolves into shared decisions, supported not by compliance but by earned credibility and mutual respect.

These qualitative insights highlight an essential truth: effective governance is not merely about structure—it is about how people experience that structure. Transparency does not erase disagreement, but it transforms resistance into dialogue. It gives people a sense of clarity, fairness, and inclusion, which allows the organization to move with both speed and integrity.

Peter Drucker captures this perfectly: "The most serious mistakes are not being made as a result of wrong answers. The truly dangerous thing is asking the wrong questions."

By paying attention to the unspoken concerns, quiet resistance, and subtle cues, leadership can transform governance from a mechanism of control into a platform for trust and collaboration.

LESSONS FOR LEADERS

James Altucher advises individuals to "own the downside" of any decision. For leaders, this means anticipating the human costs of change and addressing them upfront. Kory Kogon and Suzette Blakemore caution that unofficial project managers—those leading without formal authority—must be especially mindful of ethics, because their influence depends on relationships rather than hierarchy.

GOVERNANCE AS AN ETHICAL TOOL

Governance structures such as charters, change boards, and risk registers are sometimes viewed as bureaucratic hurdles. However, in the right hands, they become safeguards for dignity. Clear documentation reduces rumor-driven anxiety. Scheduled feedback sessions provide a predictable forum for concerns. Transparent communication builds a bridge between leadership and staff.

This approach embodies a simple truth: the ability to work effectively with people is as critical as technical competence. Ethical governance isn't just about compliance; it's about creating trust in the process.

Ethical change is not a luxury; it is a strategic necessity. By embedding consent, transparency, and respect into PMO practices, organizations can show that projectization doesn't have to come at the expense of dignity.

In a project economy where teams form and dissolve rapidly, leaders who prioritize humanity alongside performance will not only deliver results but also build the trust required for sustainable success. Ethics and efficiency are not opposing forces—they are two sides of effective leadership.

KEY TAKEAWAYS

1. Projectization Is a Human Experience, Not Just a Structural One

- Behind every process, charter, and schedule are people whose careers, identities, and well-being are impacted.
- Ethical engagement is just as critical to PMO success as technical execution.
- Lasting change requires earning trust, not just enforcing compliance.

2. Ethical Foundations Strengthen Organizational Change

- **Informed Consent:** Employees must understand what is changing and have a voice before decisions are finalized.
- **Transparency:** Open communication on decisions, metrics, and resource allocation reduces rumors and resistance.
- **Respect for Autonomy:** Teams thrive when they can shape processes that affect them.
- **Equity and Inclusion:** Fair opportunities build trust and strengthen organizational culture.

3. Practical Mechanisms Anchor Ethical Principles

- Open forums and Q&A sessions give staff direct access to leadership.

- Feedback loops — including surveys and structured conversations — turn communication into dialogue.
- Clear policies on data use ensure people understand how information about their work is collected and shared.
- These mechanisms turn values into visible actions.

4. Speed Must Be Balanced with Psychological Safety

- Rapid launches can unintentionally create pressure, exclusion, or mistrust.
- Requiring stakeholder acknowledgment in project charters ensures people are seen and heard before execution begins.
- Balancing urgency with dignity builds sustainable momentum.

5. Trust Is Earned Through Transparency and Consistency

- Employees don't need to agree with every decision— but they need to understand how decisions are made.
- When leadership listens, explains, and acknowledges feedback, trust in the process grows.
- This trust is a performance accelerator, turning resistance into cooperation.

6. Ethics Transforms Governance from Control to Collaboration

- Clear documentation, scheduled feedback, and visible decision-making reduce anxiety and build trust.

- Governance tools (charters, CCBs, risk registers) are not bureaucratic by nature—they become ethical safeguards when applied with transparency.
- As Peter Drucker observed, "The truly dangerous thing is asking the wrong questions." Listening for unspoken concerns is as important as formal reporting.

7. Leadership Means Owning the Downside

- Ethical leadership anticipates the human costs of change and addresses them proactively.
- James Altucher's call to "own the downside" reminds leaders to manage impacts, not just outputs.
- Kory Kogon and Suzette Blakemore's work highlights that unofficial project leaders rely on trust, not authority—making ethics non-negotiable.

8. Culture Is Built Through Trust, Not Directives

- Top-down mandates can enforce compliance but rarely inspire commitment.
- Ethical change involves co-creation, feedback, and shared ownership.
- When people trust the process, projectization moves from being "management's system" to "our system."

9. Ethics Is a Strategic Advantage

- In fast-moving, projectized environments, human-centered leadership creates resilience and long-term performance.
- Ethics and efficiency are not opposing forces; they reinforce each other.

- Leaders who prioritize consent, transparency, and dignity build organizations that can adapt faster and last longer.

PART FOUR
LEADING THE WORK

1

PROJECT LEADERSHIP
FROM FORMING TO PERFORMING

Projects do not succeed by methodology alone. Tools and charters set the framework, but it is leadership that converts plans into results. Whether leading a small internal effort or a multi-million-dollar infrastructure upgrade, the ability to guide a team through uncertainty and complexity is what separates competent project managers from transformative leaders.

UNDERSTANDING TEAM DYNAMICS

Bruce Tuckman's classic model of team development, "Forming, Storming, Norming, and Performing," remains a powerful lens for project leaders to understand how teams evolve:

1. Forming: Team members meet, roles are unclear, and excitement mixes with anxiety. Leaders must clarify purpose, set expectations, and create psychological safety.

2. Storming: Conflicts surface as individuals test boundaries. Effective leaders facilitate open dialogue, mediate disputes, and keep the team focused on shared objectives.
3. Norming: The team establishes working agreements, and trust grows. Leaders reinforce positive behaviors and begin to delegate more authority.
4. Performing: The team operates with high autonomy and delivers results with minimal supervision. Leaders shift from directing to coaching and removing external barriers.

Recognizing the natural tension of the storming phase allows project leaders to address issues proactively rather than misinterpreting conflict as failure. High-performing teams are built through intentional leadership, not by accident.

CORE LEADERSHIP PRINCIPLES

Stephen Covey's *7 Habits of Highly Effective People* provides timeless guidance for effective project leadership:

- Be Proactive: Anticipate risks and act before problems escalate.
- Begin with the End in Mind: Keep the mission and success criteria visible in every meeting.
- Seek First to Understand, Then to Be Understood: Listen to team concerns before prescribing solutions.
- Synergize: Leverage diverse skills and viewpoints to create better outcomes than any individual could achieve.
- Sharpen the Saw: Model continuous learning and self-care to sustain energy over long projects.

These principles encourage leaders to focus on people first, ensuring that processes support human performance rather than the other way around.

PRACTICAL LEADERSHIP TACTICS

- Vision Casting: Start each project with a compelling narrative that explains why the work matters. Lee Iacocca often reminded his teams, "The ability to concentrate and to use your time well is everything." A clear vision channels that concentration.
- Meeting Facilitation: Open every meeting with a statement of desired outcomes. Use time boxes and visible action trackers to maintain momentum.
- Conflict Resolution: Treat conflict as data. Surface disagreements early, separate people from problems, and seek win-win solutions.
- Motivation: Recognize contributions publicly. Small, frequent acknowledgments build morale and engagement.
- Decision Clarity: Summarize key decisions and owners within 24 hours to prevent ambiguity and drift.

These tactics give structure to the soft skills of leadership, translating intent into daily behaviors that build trust and maintain momentum.

LEADING WITHOUT TITLE

Kory Kogon and Suzette Blakemore emphasize that leadership is a behavior, not a job title. Many of the most impactful project initiatives are led by unofficial project managers, individuals who guide cross-disciplinary efforts without formal authority.

These leaders rely on influence, credibility, and relationship-building rather than positional power. They create alignment through clarity, remove friction, and become the connective tissue between diverse functional groups.

TECHNOLOGY AS A LEADERSHIP AMPLIFIER

Collaboration tools offer real-time visibility and speed up coordination, but technology alone cannot motivate a team. Leaders must set explicit norms for tool usage, defining which channels are for decisions, which are for discussion, and how quickly responses are expected.

Establishing digital etiquette prevents confusion, misalignment, and burnout. Technology amplifies strong leadership but can also expose weak leadership when norms are unclear.

CASE EXAMPLE: DEPENDENCY STAND-UPS

Weekly dependency stand-ups became a cornerstone of effective leadership practice. By keeping these meetings short, focused on cross-team blockers, and decision-oriented, leaders model respect for time while reinforcing accountability and shared ownership.

This approach builds a cadence of clarity and a predictable rhythm, where teams know when and how obstacles will be surfaced and resolved.

LESSONS IN LEADERSHIP

Experienced project leaders report that the most effective leadership tactic is consistent, transparent communication. One project manager reflects, "When people understand the why, they'll figure out the how."

This insight aligns with James Altucher's idea of becoming an "idea machine"—empowering teams to generate solutions rather than prescribing every step. Great leaders create space for creativity, not just control.

Project leadership is the art of guiding people through complexity. Frameworks like Tuckman's stages and Covey's habits provide structure, but daily behaviors, such as listening, clarifying, recognizing, and adapting, bring those principles to life.

As Jack Welch once said, "Good business leaders create a vision, articulate the vision, passionately own the vision, and relentlessly drive it to completion."

Leadership is ultimately about action and ownership.

In the project economy, doing something means creating an environment where teams can move from forming to performing with confidence, clarity, and shared purpose.

KEY TAKEAWAYS

1. Leadership Converts Plans into Results

- Methodology alone does not drive success— leadership bridges the gap between structure and execution.

- Tools, charters, and schedules provide the framework, but it is leadership behaviors that turn intent into measurable outcomes.
- In a project economy defined by speed and complexity, the ability to guide people effectively is a core differentiator.

2. Team Development Is Predictable—and Leadable

- Bruce Tuckman's stages—Forming, Storming, Norming, Performing—offer a reliable roadmap for understanding team evolution.
  - *Forming:* Set expectations and create psychological safety.
  - *Storming:* Normalize conflict as a natural step, not a failure.
  - *Norming:* Build trust and shared rhythms.
  - *Performing:* Empower and remove barriers.
- Recognizing and managing these phases proactively allows leaders to stabilize teams faster and build high performance intentionally.

3. People Come Before Process

- Stephen Covey's 7 Habits reinforce the human-centered nature of leadership:
  - Be proactive in addressing risks.
  - Keep the end in mind to maintain alignment.
  - Seek to understand before being understood.
  - Synergize diverse perspectives.
  - Continuously sharpen the saw.
- Leadership grounded in empathy and trust creates the conditions for sustained performance.

4. Practical Leadership Tactics Create Daily Momentum

- Vision Casting: Begin with a compelling "why" to unify and inspire.
- Meeting Facilitation: Start with clear outcomes, use time boxes, and end with documented decisions.
- Conflict Resolution: Treat conflict as useful data, not dysfunction.
- Motivation: Recognize contributions frequently to build morale.
- Decision Clarity: Confirm owners and next steps within 24 hours.
- These repeatable behaviors build trust, reduce ambiguity, and keep teams moving forward.

5. Leadership Is a Behavior, Not a Title

- As Kory Kogon and Suzette Blakemore emphasize, unofficial project leaders often drive the most critical initiatives.
- Leadership through influence and credibility is as powerful as positional authority.
- Those who communicate clearly, build relationships, and remove friction naturally become connective leaders in complex environments.

6. Technology Amplifies—It Doesn't Replace—Leadership

- Collaboration tools accelerate coordination but require clear digital norms to avoid misalignment.
- Leaders must define communication channels, decision pathways, and response expectations.

- Technology can expose weak leadership if norms aren't set, but it can also amplify strong leadership when clarity and trust exist.

7. Cadence of Clarity Builds Trust and Speed

- Weekly dependency stand-ups exemplify effective leadership: short, focused, decision-oriented, and consistent.
- Regular, predictable forums give teams confidence that obstacles will be surfaced and resolved, reinforcing shared accountability.

8. Empowerment Drives Innovation

- As James Altucher suggests, great leaders build "idea machines" teams that generate solutions rather than wait for instructions.
- Empowered teams solve problems faster, take ownership of results, and elevate overall project quality.

9. Leadership Is Communication in Action

- Transparent, consistent communication is the most effective leadership tactic.
- When teams understand *why* something matters, they'll figure out the *how*.
- Jack Welch's reminder is timeless: "Good business leaders create a vision, articulate the vision, passionately own the vision, and relentlessly drive it to completion."

10. From Forming to Performing Is a Journey

- Great project leaders guide teams through each stage with clarity, empathy, and discipline.
- Leadership is less about control and more about enabling, creating the environment where people can thrive.
- In the project economy, the ability to build trust, set clear direction, and remove obstacles is the true measure of leadership effectiveness.

2

CULTURE, DOCUMENTATION, AND MENTORING

Project frameworks provide structure, but culture determines whether that structure produces value. The transition to projectized work often succeeds not because of templates or tools alone, but because leaders intentionally cultivate a culture of openness, knowledge sharing, and mentorship. In *The Trillion Dollar Coach*, Bill Campbell's legacy centered on shaping culture through leadership behaviors rather than policy manuals. He believed that leaders are first and foremost coaches, setting expectations, building trust, and developing people. Great frameworks work best when leaders make culture personal and visible.

THE POWER OF CULTURE

Culture is the sum of everyday behaviors, not a slogan or a poster on the wall. Stephen Covey described culture as the "collective habits" of an organization. When those habits favor transparency and respect, projects thrive. When they lean toward secrecy or blame, even the best processes fracture under pressure.

Strong project cultures foster psychological safety, an environment where team members feel free to surface risks, admit mistakes, and challenge assumptions without fear of retaliation. This kind of openness is particularly critical in complex initiatives, where early disclosure of issues can save significant time, cost, and credibility. Bill Campbell coached executives to create environments where candor was safe and expected. He often said the job of a leader isn't to avoid conflict but to make hard conversations constructive. In high-performing cultures, leaders model vulnerability and directness, making psychological safety real, not theoretical.

Lee Iacocca captured the principle succinctly: "The ability to get along with people is as important as being technically competent." Effective leaders create environments where collaboration is not forced but naturally reinforced through everyday interactions.

Practical Cultural Practices:

- Open Reviews: Portfolio meetings function as conversations rather than interrogations, encouraging teams to share lessons learned alongside successes.
- Voice Equity: Facilitators ensure that junior contributors and senior experts alike have opportunities to speak and be heard.
- Celebrating Micro-Wins: Leaders highlight small accomplishments to reinforce positive behaviors and sustain momentum.

Bill Campbell was famous for walking around, celebrating people, and noticing the little things that mattered. He understood that leadership isn't only expressed in boardrooms but also in everyday interactions—how leaders listen, give feedback, and show up.

DOCUMENTATION AS KNOWLEDGE INFRASTRUCTURE

While culture sets the tone, documentation preserves knowledge. Projects begin and end, but well-crafted records enable continuity long after the team disbands. Kory Kogon and Suzette Blakemore remind us that "what isn't documented can't be transferred."

Many high-performing organizations adopt lightweight yet structured documentation standards to capture both processes and insights, ensuring critical knowledge doesn't disappear when people move on or projects end. Typical artifacts include:

- Project Charters: One-page summaries outlining purpose, scope, and key milestones.
- Risk Registers: Living documents tracking potential issues and mitigation strategies.
- Decision Logs: Concise records of critical choices, rationale, and responsible parties.
- Lessons Learned Canvases: Post-project templates capturing what worked, what didn't, and what to do differently next time.

These artifacts are most powerful when stored in shared, well-organized digital repositories with intuitive naming conventions and role-based access. The objective isn't to create documentation for its own sake; it's to build a durable knowledge infrastructure that supports future teams, accelerates onboarding, and reduces rework.

THE RISKS OF RELYING ON TRIBAL KNOWLEDGE

Organizations that lean too heavily on tribal knowledge, the unwritten, informal know-how stored in people's heads, often experience operational drag, knowledge silos, and fragility in their delivery processes. While informal knowledge networks can make teams nimble in the short term, over time, they introduce significant strategic and operational risks:

1. Single Points of Failure

When only a few key individuals know critical processes or system configurations, their absence—whether due to turnover, leave, or reassignment—can stall entire projects. Tribal knowledge turns people into bottlenecks rather than multipliers.

2. Reinventing the Wheel

Without documented history, new teams repeatedly rebuild solutions to problems that were already solved. Valuable lessons, workarounds, and hard-won insights vanish, forcing teams to pay the same learning costs multiple times.

3. Inconsistent Execution and Quality Drift
4. Informal knowledge transfer often leads to inconsistent practices across teams. Different interpretations of "the way things are done" create quality gaps, misalignments, and prevent scaling.
5. Slower Onboarding and Ramp-Up
6. New hires often learn through shadowing or word of mouth, resulting in longer, more error-prone ramp-up times. In projectized environments with fast-

forming teams, this delays delivery and frustrates both leaders and team members.

7. Poor Decision Recall

8. Tribal knowledge erodes organizational memory. Months later, no one remembers *why* a decision was made, what trade-offs were accepted, or which dependencies were considered. This creates confusion, leads to repeated debates, and results in avoidable delays.

9. Cultural Dependence on "Heroes"

10. Relying on tribal knowledge often produces a hero culture, where a handful of veterans hold the keys to progress. While this may seem efficient, it discourages collaboration, disempowers new voices, and makes the organization brittle.

TURNING KNOWLEDGE INTO INFRASTRUCTURE

To overcome these risks, leading PMOs and engineering organizations treat documentation as a core operational asset rather than an afterthought. This means:

- Embedding documentation milestones into project lifecycles (e.g., charter sign-off, risk log updates, closeout lessons learned).
- Enforcing lightweight but mandatory standards to balance agility with clarity.
- Maintaining centralized, searchable repositories that integrate with collaboration tools.
- Rewarding documentation as a leadership behavior, not clerical work.

Bill Campbell believed great leaders remove friction so teams can focus on impact. Encouraging documentation and clarity wasn't about control; it was about empowering people to make better decisions faster. In his coaching, clear communication was a leadership *duty*, not a nice-to-have.

Peter Drucker famously noted, "What gets measured gets managed." Another way to put it is, "if you can't measure it, you can't manage it." In the same spirit, what gets documented gets preserved, and what gets preserved enables organizational learning at scale.

Bottom Line: Tribal knowledge might help teams move fast temporarily, but it anchors organizations to fragility. Documentation, by contrast, builds resilience, consistency, and clarity. In a projectized world where teams form, execute, and dissolve rapidly, knowledge infrastructure is as critical as technical infrastructure. It's what allows progress to be repeatable rather than accidental.

MENTORING AS CULTURAL GLUE

Knowledge transfer is not only about systems and documents; it is also about people. Pairing experienced staff with newcomers in informal mentoring relationships accelerates onboarding and ensures that tacit knowledge, the kind that rarely appears in manuals, is passed along. Bill Campbell's superpower was mentorship. He coached leaders to spend real time developing people, not just managing projects. In projectized environments, mentorship isn't a soft skill—it's the mechanism that scales culture and leadership.

James Altucher might call this "creating your own network effect," where each mentoring connection amplifies the team's collective capability.

Effective Mentoring Guidelines:

- Encourage reverse mentoring, allowing junior staff to share expertise in emerging technologies and fresh perspectives.
- Pair mentors and mentees across disciplines to break down functional silos.
- Recognize and reward mentors in performance evaluations to reinforce the cultural value of knowledge sharing.

INTEGRATION OF CULTURE AND DOCUMENTATION

Culture and documentation reinforce each other. A culture that values openness encourages accurate documentation, while strong documentation reduces anxiety, builds trust, and supports psychological safety.

Stephen Covey's "Sharpen the Saw" habit applies well here: organizations must continually renew their knowledge systems and mentoring practices to stay resilient and effective in a fast-moving project economy.

LESSONS FOR LEADERS

Leaders must model the behaviors they seek to institutionalize. When executives and project leads contribute to risk registers and decision logs themselves, they signal that documentation is not administrative overhead; it is leadership work. Bill Campbell believed that "you can't coach what you don't live." Leaders who coach, listen, and build trust create the cultural backbone of successful organizations. Their actions teach far more than their policies.

When leaders also act as mentors, they show that career development and knowledge transfer are strategic priorities, not afterthoughts. This visible commitment to both culture and knowledge infrastructure creates durable project environments that outlast individual contributors.

Culture enables trust. Documentation preserves wisdom. Mentoring ensures both endure. Together, they form the backbone of a sustainable project economy.

Bill Campbell's legacy reminds us that strong leadership isn't about control, it's about *care*—for the people, the team, and the mission. Leaders who coach build cultures that last far beyond individual projects.

KEY TAKEAWAYS

1. **Culture drives outcomes:** No framework succeeds without a culture of openness, trust, and shared accountability.

2. **Psychological safety matters:** Teams innovate and problem-solve more effectively when they feel safe to speak up.

3. **Documentation preserves institutional memory:** Well-structured knowledge artifacts reduce reliance on individuals and improve continuity.

4. **Mentorship multiplies impact:** Pairing experienced staff with newcomers accelerates learning and breaks down silos.

5. **Leaders must model the change:** Cultural behaviors stick when leaders participate directly in documentation, communication, and mentoring.

6. **Culture + Documentation + Mentorship = Resilience:**

These three elements together create a foundation that sustains project performance over time.

3

SCHEDULING WITHOUT TIME TRAVEL

Every project manager has seen it, the magical schedule where everything is on time, nothing ever slips, and tasks always start *exactly* when planned. It looks perfect on paper . . . but reality has a way of showing up like a time travel paradox.

A task "scheduled" to start next month is already underway. Another task shows as "100% complete" even though its finish date is still a week away. Suddenly, your Gantt chart looks less like a plan and more like a DeLorean dashboard.

This is what I like to call "schedule time travel," when your timeline exists in an alternate universe, disconnected from the actual progress on the ground.

THE REAL PURPOSE OF A SCHEDULE

A schedule is not a work of science fiction. It's not a wish list. It's a contract of expectations between the team and its stakeholders. As Stephen Covey might say, "Begin with the

End in Mind." The purpose of the schedule is to guide delivery to that end, not to preserve an optimistic fantasy.

A good schedule does three things well:

- **Clarifies** the work and sequence of effort.
- **Surfaces** risks before they become crises.
- **Guides** decision-making in real time.

A schedule that doesn't reflect reality isn't just inaccurate, it's dangerous. It breeds complacency, erodes trust, and leaves leadership making decisions based on fiction rather than fact.

TECHNICAL FOUNDATIONS

Good scheduling isn't about complexity; it's about clarity. Some classic techniques still stand the test of time:

- **Work Breakdown Structure (WBS):** Break the project into manageable chunks so everyone knows what's in play.
- **Critical Path Method (CPM):** Identify the sequence of tasks that *actually determines* how long the project will take.
- **Float/Slack Analysis:** Know where you can absorb a delay and where you can't.
- **Buffers and Contingencies:** Add time cushions to absorb the real world's favorite trick—surprises.

These fundamentals anchor your plan in reality, not alternate timelines.

PRACTICAL HABITS FOR REALISTIC FORECASTING

- **Effort-Driven Estimates**: Base durations on actual hours and available resources, not wishful thinking.
- **Progressive Elaboration**: Refine as you go. A living schedule is allowed to *grow* as more is learned.
- **Short Task Durations**: Break work into chunks small enough to measure within each reporting cycle.
- **Regular Updates**: A schedule that isn't updated regularly turns into a time machine, and not the cool kind.
- **Transparent Variances**: Report the truth early. A slipped task is manageable; a buried one is catastrophic.

James Altucher often says, "Iterate in small bets." The same logic applies here: frequent, honest adjustments beat long stretches of fantasy planning.

WHEN TIME TRAVEL HAPPENS

Schedules slip. Deliveries stall. Dependencies fall out of sync. The real leadership moment comes when you communicate those variances early and clearly.

Think of it like turbulence on a flight. Passengers get nervous if the cockpit stays silent. However, a calm voice explaining what's happening restores confidence.

When reality drifts from plan:

- Surface the variance immediately.
- Explain *why* it happened.

- Propose options for mitigation.
- Adjust the schedule so the artifact matches the truth.

A schedule that reflects actual status—not what was *supposed* to happen—is the only kind that deserves trust.

TOOLS AND TECHNOLOGY

Modern tools like Microsoft Project, Primavera, and Smartsheet make it easy to see critical path impacts in real time, but tools alone don't prevent time travel.

Pair predictive schedules with visual boards (Kanban, sprint boards, dashboards) that show what's happening *now*. When the two match, you have clarity. When they don't, you have a paradox to fix.

HUMAN FACTORS

The real battle isn't fought on the timeline; it's fought in the culture.

Team members need to feel safe saying, "Hey, this started early," or "We're behind." Without psychological safety, people will quietly adjust reality to fit the schedule, rather than adjust the schedule to fit reality.

Trust > Fiction. Always.

FUN WITH TIME TRAVEL: THE "PARADOX" EXAMPLE

Picture this:

- **Task X** was scheduled to start next Friday. But . . . it started yesterday.
- **Task Y** is already marked "complete," but the finish date is next Tuesday.

Congratulations—your project just invented a time machine. But instead of flux capacitors, it's powered by bad data.

Leaders who tolerate these paradoxes end up managing ghosts —work that happened or didn't happen in the wrong timeline. And ghost work doesn't get you across the finish line.

The fix is simple:

- Update the start date.
- Adjust the finish date.
- Let the timeline tell the *true story.*

Scheduling without time travel requires a mix of technical rigor, honest communication, and cultural trust.

- Critical path analysis and buffers provide the mechanics.
- Frequent updates keep the timeline anchored in reality.
- Open communication builds trust around those updates.

As Lee Iacocca once said, "The ability to concentrate and to use your time well is everything." A schedule that reflects reality channels that concentration. A schedule that lives in an alternate timeline just wastes it.

KEY TAKEAWAYS

1. A schedule is a living contract, not a wish list. It must reflect what's *actually happening*—not what you *wish* would happen.

2. Time travel in scheduling (tasks starting or finishing in the future or past) erodes trust and creates decision-making blind spots.

3. Short tasks, frequent updates, and transparent variances keep the schedule anchored.

4. Tools don't fix bad data; honest communication and cultural safety do.

5. Schedule realism = leadership maturity. Fictional timelines look pretty in reports, but reality delivers results.

6. When in doubt, fix the paradox: adjust the schedule to match reality, not the other way around.

4

DEPENDENCIES AND RISK, "BEFORE THE FIRST DOMINO FALLS"

Projects rarely fail because of one spectacular disaster. More often, they falter through a slow accumulation of hidden dependencies and unmanaged risks, quietly building pressure behind the scenes until one slight delay sets off a domino effect.

A late part shipment.

A missing approval.

A resource conflict.

Each of these, on its own, may seem minor, but together, they can derail an entire timeline.

Dependency and risk management isn't just a technical discipline—it's a leadership capability that turns complexity into visibility.

UNDERSTANDING DEPENDENCIES

A dependency exists whenever the start or finish of one task depends on another. Recognizing these interconnections early allows leaders to anticipate constraints and protect the critical path.

Types of Dependencies

- Technical Dependencies: Hardware must arrive before it can be installed, and software must pass testing before deployment.
- Resource Dependencies: A specific engineer or subject matter expert is needed for multiple projects, creating sequencing issues.
- Decision Dependencies: Approvals or design sign-offs must occur before procurement or execution begins.
- External Dependencies: Third-party vendors, regulatory approvals, or customer inputs that sit outside direct team control.

Technical Tools for Managing Dependencies

- Dependency Register: A living document or board that records the dependency, its owner, target date, and impact if delayed.
- Network Diagrams: Visual task maps that clarify relationships, critical path items, and choke points.
- Interface Control Documents (ICDs): Formal agreements between teams or systems to define interaction points and responsibilities.

Practical Dependency Tactics

- Weekly Dependency Stand-Ups: Short, focused, cross-team meetings where each team reports what changed, what's blocking, and what decisions are needed.
- Color-Coded Dashboards: Simple visual cues—red, yellow, green—highlighting dependencies most likely to impact milestones.
- Early Warning Signals: Encouraging team members to raise flags *before* deadlines are missed. "Early is good; late is expensive."

Dependencies are leading indicators of risk. If managed properly, they give you time to react. If ignored, they turn into crises.

RISK MANAGEMENT: PMI'S STRUCTURED APPROACH

Risk is the probability of an uncertain event that can impact project objectives positively or negatively. The Project Management Institute (PMI) formalizes this through a set of structured processes in the PMBOK® Guide:

1. Plan Risk Management: Establish how risks will be identified, analyzed, responded to, and monitored. This includes defining roles, escalation paths, thresholds, and reporting cadence.

2. Identify Risks: Document potential threats and opportunities using techniques such as brainstorming, assumption analysis, expert interviews, and checklists from past projects.

3. Perform Qualitative Risk Analysis: Prioritize risks based on probability and impact, typically using a Probability–Impact Matrix. High-priority risks get early attention.

4. Perform Quantitative Risk Analysis *(optional but powerful)*: Use numerical methods like Monte Carlo simulations, sensitivity analysis, or expected monetary value to assess overall risk exposure.

5. Plan Risk Responses: Choose appropriate strategies:

- **Avoid:** Eliminate the threat.
- **Mitigate:** Reduce the likelihood or impact.
- **Transfer:** Shift risk to another party (e.g., insurance, vendor contracts).
- **Accept:** Acknowledge and monitor the risk without active intervention.
- **Exploit, Enhance, Share:** For positive risks (opportunities).

6. Implement Risk Responses: Ensure the planned actions are executed and monitored.

7. Monitor Risks: Track risk triggers, update the risk register, and communicate changes.

Key Risk Tools:

- **Risk Register:** Central repository of all risks, their probability, impact, owner, and mitigation strategy.
- **Probability/Impact Matrix:** Prioritizes risks for action.
- **Risk Burn-Down Chart:** Tracks mitigation progress over time.

- **Risk Breakdown Structure (RBS):** Hierarchical view of risk categories.

Leadership Insight: Stephen Covey's "Be Proactive" fits risk management perfectly—the point is to see the iceberg *before* the ship hits it.

INTEGRATING DEPENDENCIES AND RISK

Dependencies and risks are often treated as separate streams in project reporting, but they are deeply intertwined.

- A delayed dependency is a realized risk.
- A fragile dependency is a potential risk.
- A critical dependency is a risk amplifier.

Practical Integration Methods

- **Linked Registers:** Connect dependency records directly to related risks in the risk register.
- **Joint Dashboards:** Display risk probability and dependency health in a single visualization for leadership reviews.
- **Impact Forecasting:** When a dependency slips, automatically update related risk scores or forecast impacts to the critical path.
- **Scenario Planning:** Use "What if?" exercises to pre-plan mitigations for the most fragile dependencies.

Example:

If a specialized piece of equipment depends on a single supplier, the dependency should appear in both:

- **Dependency Register:** "Delivery of X unit from Vendor A."
- **Risk Register:** "Vendor delay could cause a 3-week schedule impact."
- The contingency plan might involve alternative suppliers or a workaround schedule adjustment.

When these two registers "talk to each other," leaders see the *full picture,* not just isolated pieces.

COMMUNICATION AND CULTURE

All the registers and dashboards in the world mean nothing if people are afraid to **speak up**.

Dependencies and risks thrive in silence.

That's why the best project leaders institutionalize short, honest, low-friction communication loops.

A good dependency & risk review meeting focuses on:

- What changed?
- What new risks have emerged?
- What decisions are needed?
- What mitigations are working or failing?

This transforms risk management from a static compliance exercise into a living dialogue.

Lee Iacocca famously said, "Management is nothing more than motivating other people." In practice, that means creating a culture where raising risks early is celebrated rather than punished.

LESSONS FOR LEADERS

- Identify cross-team dependencies during chartering, not halfway through execution.
- Assign clear owners for every dependency and risk—ambiguity is the enemy of mitigation.
- Use both qualitative and quantitative analysis to prioritize action.
- Encourage a no-blame culture to ensure issues are raised early.
- Integrate dependencies and risks to provide a single pane of glass for decision-makers.

KEY TAKEAWAYS

1. Dependencies are leading indicators of risk. Ignoring them is like ignoring cracks in a dam; they may seem small, but they signal bigger problems downstream.

2. PMI's structured risk processes—planning, identifying, analyzing, responding to, and monitoring risks—provide a disciplined framework for managing uncertainty.

3. Integrating dependency and risk tracking gives project leaders a clearer, more actionable view of the project landscape. A delayed dependency is not just a schedule slip—it's a risk coming to life.

4. Linked dashboards, registers, and review cadences enable leaders to act before problems snowball, turning potential crises into manageable adjustments.

5. Assign clear ownership for every dependency and risk. Ambiguity is the enemy of effective mitigation.

6. Cultivate a no-blame culture. Team members must feel safe raising early warnings without fear of repercussions.

7. Short, focused communication loops (e.g., weekly dependency stand-ups) are more effective than lengthy meetings or stale reports.

8. Proactive leadership prevents cascading failures. Catching and addressing one fragile dependency early can save weeks— or even months—of recovery later.

9. Tools are only as good as the conversations they support. Dashboards and registers work best when paired with honest, timely communication.

10. Build your own runway. As James Altucher says, proactive preparation gives your team the flexibility to navigate turbulence rather than react to it.

PART FIVE
LEADING THE WORK

1

AI, AUTOMATION, AND THE FUTURE OF PROJECT MANAGEMENT

Artificial intelligence is no longer a futuristic concept—it's a present reality that's redefining how projects are planned, executed, and monitored. From automated scheduling to predictive risk analysis, AI offers tools that can dramatically improve speed, precision, and decision-making quality.

However, as technology advances, the role of human judgment, creativity, and leadership becomes more, not less, critical. The future of project management will belong to those who can combine machine intelligence with human insight, using each for what it does best.

EMERGING TECHNOLOGIES

AI now supports nearly every stage of the project lifecycle:

- **Predictive Scheduling:** Algorithms analyze historical performance, task interdependencies, and resource data to forecast completion dates and flag likely delays before they occur.

- **Automated Reporting:** Natural language processing (NLP) generates real-time status reports, meeting notes, and risk summaries—freeing project managers from manual documentation.
- **Resource Optimization:** Machine learning models dynamically suggest staffing changes based on workload fluctuations, availability, and skills, helping balance cost with capacity.
- **Risk Detection:** AI scans communications, schedules, and project artifacts to detect early warning signs of cost overruns, missed milestones, or scope creep.
- **Decision Support Dashboards:** Integrated AI dashboards synthesize complex data streams into actionable insights, allowing leaders to prioritize interventions with clarity.

Practical Example

Many organizations now use AI-assisted forecasting tools to predict hardware delivery delays, supply chain constraints, or network disruptions.

Instead of discovering the problem after it happens, project leaders receive early signals—allowing them to re-baseline schedules, communicate upstream impacts, and reallocate resources before risks turn into emergencies.

This is not about replacing project managers. It's about giving them enhanced human situational awareness.

THE HUMAN ADVANTAGE

Despite AI's impressive capabilities, technology cannot replicate the uniquely human aspects of leadership. Tools can surface data, but people must interpret, prioritize, and act on it.

Stephen Covey's leadership habits, "Seek First to Understand," "Think Win-Win," and "Sharpen the Saw," remain essential, especially in AI-augmented environments.

Key human leadership strengths include:

- Ethical Judgment: Determining when to rely on algorithmic recommendations and when to override them.
- Stakeholder Engagement: Building trust around data-driven decisions.
- Creative Problem Solving: Addressing issues that algorithms can't model—such as politics, culture, or unexpected organizational shifts.
- Motivation and Coaching: Inspiring teams to embrace change and innovate without fear.

BALANCED PRACTICES: HUMAN IN THE LOOP

Successful AI adoption requires blending technology with human oversight:

- Automated risk detection informs weekly stand-ups.
- AI-driven insights shape dashboards and forecasts.
- Human teams evaluate context, assign priorities, and make the final calls.

This "human in the loop" model ensures that data informs decisions—but doesn't dictate them. It also creates accountability and transparency, two factors AI cannot provide on its own.

OPPORTUNITIES AND RISKS

AI in project management offers remarkable advantages:

- Faster decision cycles
- More accurate forecasts
- Earlier risk detection
- Reduced administrative burden

However, it also introduces new dimensions of risk:

- **Data Privacy:** Sensitive information may flow through automated systems that must be secured.
- **Algorithmic Bias:** If AI learns from biased data, it can reinforce inequities or flawed assumptions.
- **Transparency:** AI must be explainable to stakeholders—especially when decisions impact cost, schedule, or personnel.

Jack Welch once said, "Control your own destiny or someone else will." For project leaders, that destiny now includes understanding AI well enough to ask the right questions, challenge flawed outputs, and apply insights responsibly.

PREPARING FOR THE FUTURE

James Altucher's advice to become an "idea machine" applies directly here. Tomorrow's project leaders must:

- Stay fluent in emerging AI trends and tools.
- Experiment with automation to identify where it adds value.
- Sharpen soft skills that machines cannot replicate—like negotiation, empathy, and vision.

- Understand enough technical detail to challenge or validate AI outputs effectively.

The winning project manager of the future is not a coder or a robot—they are a translator, bridging intelligent machines and human mission.

The future of project management is not human versus machine; it's human plus machine.

AI will handle the heavy lifting of data collection, analysis, and reporting. Human leaders will provide the vision, ethics, and empathy needed to turn insights into impact.

Those who master this partnership will lead projects that are not only faster and smarter—but more trusted, transparent, and resilient.

KEY TAKEAWAYS

1. AI enhances, not replaces, project leadership. It frees managers from routine tasks and gives them sharper foresight.

2. Predictive tools and automated reporting can identify risks and delays far earlier than traditional methods.

3. Human judgment remains irreplaceable. Ethics, empathy, and contextual problem solving are uniquely human strengths.

4. "Human in the loop" models ensure AI supports decision-making without removing accountability.

5. AI adoption introduces new risks; data privacy, bias, and transparency must be managed deliberately.

6. Leaders must learn AI literacy. Not to become data

scientists, but to ask better questions and challenge assumptions.

7. Balanced integration of AI and people results in faster decisions, clearer forecasts, and stronger stakeholder trust.

8. Continuous learning is essential. Staying ahead of technology shifts will define future-ready project leaders.

9. Project managers are translators. Their role is to connect intelligent systems to human goals.

10. Human plus machine is the winning formula. This synergy turns technology into a competitive advantage, not a threat.

2

STANDING UP A PMO AND CHANGE BOARD

Launching a Project Management Office (PMO) is both a technical project and a leadership exercise. The goal is to create a structure that standardizes project practices, provides portfolio visibility, and supports decision-making—without becoming a bureaucratic burden. A PMO's success comes from blending disciplined implementation steps with a culture of collaboration and trust.

PURPOSE AND VISION

A PMO exists to increase the organization's ability to deliver value through projects. Leaders must clearly articulate why the PMO matters. Leaders need to support their words with actions that demonstrate the PMO is improving delivery predictability, enabling cross-team collaboration, or aligning projects with strategic goals. A compelling vision, backed by actions, helps secure executive sponsorship and employee buy-in.

IMPLEMENTATION STEPS

1. **Charter the PMO:** Define its mission, services, and success metrics. Keep the charter concise and action-oriented.
2. **Start Small:** Launch with a pilot set of projects to demonstrate quick wins and refine processes.
3. **Standardize Core Templates:** Provide charters, risk registers, and status reports to create a common language.
4. **Establish Governance:** Create a Change Control Board (CCB) to evaluate scope changes, manage dependencies, and approve resource adjustments.
5. **Set Cadence:** Schedule weekly dependency stand-ups, monthly portfolio reviews, and quarterly process retrospectives.
6. **Measure and Adjust:** Track throughput, forecast accuracy, and stakeholder satisfaction. Use data to iterate on PMO practices.

LEADERSHIP AND CULTURAL CONSIDERATIONS

Stephen Covey's habits provide a leadership framework:

- Seek First to Understand: Engage stakeholders early to understand their concerns about the added process.
- Think Win-Win: Position the PMO as a partner that simplifies work, not as a gatekeeper.
- Synergize: Combine input from engineering, finance, and operations to design flexible templates.

- Sharpen the Saw: Invest in ongoing training to build project management capabilities across the organization.

Case Example: NAS Change Board

NAS implemented a lightweight Change Control Board that meets biweekly to review proposed changes and major risks. The board includes PMO leaders, technical experts, and key stakeholders. Meetings are capped at 30 minutes, with decisions logged in a shared repository for full transparency. This simple structure ensures that critical changes receive timely, documented approval without slowing down projects.

Practical Tips for a Successful Launch

- Communicate Early and Often: Share progress updates and invite feedback to reduce resistance.
- Celebrate Early Wins: Publicize the first successful projects to demonstrate PMO value.
- Keep Tools Simple: Start with accessible platforms (like spreadsheets or SharePoint) before introducing specialized software.
- Empower Unofficial Project Managers: Provide coaching for team leads who manage projects without formal authority.

LESSONS LEARNED

The PMO will earn credibility by delivering tangible value quickly. Within the first year, leadership will see improved forecast accuracy, faster decision cycles, and greater stakeholder satisfaction. As Steve Jobs once said, "Innovation distinguishes between a leader and a follower." By building internal capabilities early, the organization will position itself to lead the change rather than be forced to follow it.

Standing up a PMO and Change Board is not simply about installing templates; it is about creating a culture of accountability and collaboration. By combining disciplined implementation steps with intentional leadership, organizations can establish a PMO that enhances project performance without stifling innovation.

KEY TAKEAWAYS

1. A PMO is both a structure and a leadership initiative. It standardizes project delivery, improves visibility, and supports decision-making—while relying on trust, communication, and shared ownership to succeed.

2. A clear purpose and vision are critical for buy-in. Executives and staff must understand *why* the PMO exists and *how* it will make their work easier, not harder.

3. Start small and scale deliberately. Launching with pilot projects and lightweight tools builds early credibility and allows for rapid iteration.

4. Core templates create a common language. Standardized charters, risk registers, and status reports reduce friction and make governance more transparent.

5. Change Control Boards (CCBs) enable disciplined agility. A simple, time-boxed CCB process ensures critical changes are reviewed and documented without slowing progress.

6. Cadence drives consistency. Regular stand-ups, portfolio reviews, and retrospectives build rhythm, visibility, and accountability into the organization.

7. Leadership behaviors shape PMO culture. Applying principles like "Seek First to Understand" and "Think Win-Win" fosters partnership over policing.

8. Early wins build momentum. Demonstrating measurable value—such as improved forecast accuracy and faster decisions—accelerates trust and adoption.

9. Keep tools simple at the start. Overly complex systems can stall adoption. Start with accessible solutions and scale capabilities as the PMO matures.

10. Empower unofficial project managers. Supporting team leads who manage projects informally expands PMO influence and strengthens delivery capacity across the organization.

11. Innovation and leadership go hand in hand. As Steve Jobs said, "Innovation distinguishes between a leader and a follower." By building internal PMO capabilities early, organizations position themselves to lead change—not chase it.

12. Culture is the real differentiator. A successful PMO isn't just about templates and reports—it's about enabling people to work together effectively and deliver value predictably.

3

PURPOSE–VIEW ALIGNMENT & TASK–TECHNOLOGY FIT

Technology can accelerate or slow down projects, depending on how well it aligns with the project's purpose and the needs of its users. In the project economy, selecting the right tools is as much a strategic leadership decision as a technical one. A Project Management Office (PMO) must come to realize that the best technology is not always the most feature-rich, but the one that best fits the project's purpose, stakeholder expectations, and team workflows.

Legendary NFL coach Bill Walsh built a dynasty not by focusing on the scoreboard, but by perfecting the standards of performance, a set of behaviors, principles, and operational clarity that ensured excellence in every detail. As he famously said, "The score takes care of itself." In the same way, if a PMO establishes clarity of purpose and aligns technology precisely to that purpose, the metrics of on-time delivery, cost control, and stakeholder satisfaction tend to follow naturally.

LINKING PURPOSE TO VIEW

Stephen Covey's habit of "Begin with the End in Mind" provides the foundation for tool selection. Leaders must first clarify the project's purpose and the outcomes stakeholders expect. Only then can they determine which "view" of information, dashboards, reports, or interactive boards, will best communicate progress and enable decisions.

A well-designed project information view acts like a quarterback's field vision: it allows the team to see what matters, when it matters. Bill Walsh taught his players that precision in preparation creates freedom in execution. Likewise, clarity in information design and visibility allow project teams to execute with speed and confidence.

When tools are selected reactively or based on trend appeal, they often clutter rather than clarify. However, when tools are deliberately aligned with the mission, stakeholder perspective, and decision cadence, they create focus. As Jocko Willink reminds us in Extreme Ownership, "Discipline equals freedom." Discipline in technology selection and use unlocks operational agility.

Strategic Alignment Checklist

- **Mission Clarity:** What outcome are we trying to achieve, and who needs to see progress?
- **Stakeholder Needs:** Do executives require portfolio-level dashboards while engineers need detailed task boards?
- **Decision Cadence:** How often will the data drive decisions like daily stand-ups, weekly reviews, or quarterly planning?

Purpose-to-view alignment is also a leadership act. Eric Schmidt, in Trillion Dollar Coach, describes how Bill Campbell coached leaders at Google, Apple, and Intuit to make sure teams had "the right conversations with the right people at the right time." The right technology view enables those conversations—not just status reports, but decision-enabling dialogue.

TASK–TECHNOLOGY FIT

Once the purpose and view are clear, the next step is to match tasks to technology. This ensures the chosen tool is not only visionary but operationally useful.

For example, NASA NAS evaluated tools like Jira, Smartsheet, and SharePoint based on their ability to support specific tasks, such as risk tracking, schedule forecasting, and dependency mapping. The key question was not "What's the best tool?" but rather "Which tool best supports the tasks required to deliver mission outcomes?"

Evaluation Rubric

- **Ease of Use:** Can non-technical stakeholders access and understand the data?
- **Integration:** Does the tool connect with existing systems for data sharing?
- **Scalability:** Will it handle future growth in projects and users?
- **Security & Compliance:** Does it meet organizational and federal security standards?
- **Cost vs. Value:** Are the benefits worth the licensing and maintenance expenses?

Practical Selection Process

- **Define Critical Tasks:** Identify the core activities the tool must support (e.g., change control, resource allocation, risk tracking).
- **Pilot the Options:** Run a short proof-of-concept with a small project team to gather feedback.
- **Gather Stakeholder Input:** Include end users in the evaluation to ensure adoption.
- **Decide and Train:** Select the tool that best fits the tasks and provide targeted training sessions.

A PMO should evaluate project management tools through a structured, criteria-driven process rather than relying on convenience, vendor marketing, or legacy systems.

This process reflects the Extreme Ownership mindset: leaders don't blame tools for failure; they ensure the right tool is selected, adopted, and used effectively. As Willink writes, "Leaders must own everything in their world. There is no one else to blame." When projects stall because tools are poorly matched, it's not a technology problem; it's a leadership gap.

BEYOND POPULARITY: STRATEGIC FIT OVER TREND

It is common for individuals to champion a particular project management tool simply because it worked well in another organization. However, a tool's past success elsewhere does not guarantee its success here. Every environment has its own operational tempo, cultural dynamics, and governance expectations.

To borrow a sports analogy: many professional quarterbacks have struggled in one team's offensive system, only to thrive when placed in a scheme better suited to their style of play. The same holds true for project management solutions; their effectiveness depends on how well they align with the environment in which they are deployed.

HUMAN FACTORS: THE DECISIVE VARIABLE

James Altucher warns against chasing shiny objects. A flashy tool that fails to align with daily workflows can create more work than it saves. Kory Kogon and Suzette Blakemore emphasize the importance of training and change management so that the selected technology becomes a productivity multiplier rather than a source of frustration.

No matter how technically sound a platform may be, its success or failure often depends on how well leaders communicate expectations and coach adoption. Bill Campbell's philosophy from Trillion Dollar Coach is instructive here: "It's the people." Technology amplifies human behavior; it doesn't replace it.

Jocko Willink makes a similar point in Extreme Ownership: tools are force multipliers, but only when teams are disciplined and aligned. An undisciplined team with great tools will underperform. A disciplined team with average tools can excel. Leadership, not technology, is the decisive variable.

TOOL GOVERNANCE AS LEADERSHIP WORK

Too often, governance is seen as an administrative burden. In reality, tool governance is leadership in action. When leaders shape how information flows, how decisions are made, and how tasks are coordinated through a platform, they set the organization's operational rhythm.

LESSONS FROM ELITE TEAMS AND WINNING CULTURES

Elite sports teams and high-performing tech organizations share a principle: clarity of systems beats complexity of tools.

Bill Walsh built dynasties through systems that everyone understood. Eric Schmidt's Google thrived by pairing coaching leadership with clear operational platforms. Jocko Willink's SEAL teams executed missions successfully because the technology and processes were laser-aligned to their purpose.

Leaders in PMOs should see themselves not as tool buyers, but as system architects and coaches.

Lessons Learned

- Start with purpose, not features.
- Engage stakeholders early to define information needs.
- Pilot tools with real projects before enterprise rollout.
- Provide ongoing training and feedback loops to ensure sustained adoption.
- Lead from the front. When leaders use and respect the system, teams follow.
- Avoid shiny object syndrome. A clean fit beats flashy features every time.

Technology should serve the project, not the other way around. By aligning purpose with the right view and ensuring that tasks fit the chosen technology, leaders can create a tool ecosystem that enhances communication, accelerates delivery, and builds trust across all levels of the organization.

This is not simply a technical decision; it is a leadership practice. Bill Campbell coached some of the world's best technology executives to make their platforms serve people and mission, not ego or convenience. Jocko Willink calls this taking ownership. Bill Walsh showed us that disciplined systems, executed well, bring predictable excellence.

As Lee Iacocca advised, "The ability to concentrate and to use your time well is everything." The right tools let teams focus on value creation, not tool maintenance.

KEY TAKEAWAYS

1. Start with Purpose, Not Tools: The effectiveness of any project management technology depends on how well it aligns with the project's mission, stakeholder needs, and decision cadence—not on how many features it offers.

2. Clarify Information Views: Different stakeholders need different perspectives. Executives may require strategic dashboards, while delivery teams need tactical task boards. Matching the view to the audience drives better decisions.

3. Ensure Task–Technology Fit: Technology should seamlessly support core activities such as risk tracking, scheduling, and dependency mapping. A misaligned tool can become an obstacle rather than an enabler.

4. Evaluate Objectively, Not Emotionally: A tool that worked well in another organization may not fit your operational environment. Strategic fit matters more than popularity.

5. Pilot Before Full Rollout: Testing tools with small, real-world projects reveals adoption barriers and integration gaps early, allowing smarter decisions.

6. Prioritize Human Adoption: Even the best tools fail without proper training, communication, and change management. Technology must support people—not replace their judgment.

7. Reinforce Governance and Transparency: The selected solution should enhance visibility, streamline decision-making, and integrate smoothly into existing governance structures.

8. Stay Focused on Value Creation: The ultimate goal of any tool is to enable clarity, accelerate delivery, and free teams to focus on meaningful work—not tool maintenance.

4

MICRO-PIVOTS: PATTERNS FOR DAY-TO-DAY WINS

Large transformations often capture headlines, but lasting progress is usually built through small, consistent adjustments and micro-pivots that accumulate over time. In the project economy, where teams must adapt quickly to shifting priorities, mastering these small moves can deliver outsized results.

The Mindset of Continuous Improvement

The leadership thinker Stephen Covey offers one of the most enduring mindsets: "Sharpen the Saw"—the idea that we must constantly renew ourselves in mind, body, and work. Micro-pivots embody this principle. Rather than waiting for quarterly reviews or major reorganizations, teams make small, frequent changes to processes, communication patterns, and workflows. As James Altucher puts it, this is "iterating in small bets"—testing ideas quickly, learning from feedback, and scaling what works.

By placing micro-pivots at the heart of the day-to-day rhythm, organizations move from reactive to proactive. Rather than saying, "We'll fix it in next quarter's transformation," teams say, "Let's try this now and learn." That shift in mindset is what separates high-velocity organizations from those stuck in analysis paralysis.

In agile frameworks, micro-pivots are natural. Scrum teams hold daily stand-ups, sprint retrospectives, and backlog grooming sessions before each iteration—these are micro-pivots in action. A team may, for example, decide mid-sprint to swap out a user story because early testing reveals the user value differs from what was assumed. That quick shift saves wasted effort and keeps momentum. Agile leadership emphasizes that "Inspect and adapt" isn't just a retrospective tagline—it's a living practice.

WHY MICRO-PIVOTS MATTER

Here are some of the key benefits of adopting micro-pivots:

- **Speed of adaptation**: Small adjustments can be made in hours or days, avoiding the long lead time of significant change initiatives.
- **Reduced risk**: Because the change is small and reversible, teams can experiment without major disruption.
- **Learning orientation**: Frequent small changes embed reflection loops and accelerate feedback cycles.
- **Cultural reinforcement**: When micro-pivots become routine, they reinforce a culture of continuous improvement rather than fear of change.
- **Compounding effects**: Like compound interest, small gains add up. Over a year, 5–10%

improvements each month lead to material shifts in performance.

Seen in this light, micro-pivots are not trivial; they are strategic. They are the "low drag" version of change management. Instead of waiting for the next big program, teams keep moving.

DAILY PRACTICES FOR MICRO-PIVOTS

Here are some practical patterns to embed micro-pivot capability into your working rhythm:

- **Five-Slide Vision Deck**
- Start every project with a concise deck that summarizes purpose, value, scope, milestones, and key risks. But don't let it sit static. Update it regularly —say biweekly or monthly—to reflect what's changed. This keeps the "north star" alive and surfaces small shifts early.
- **One-Page Status Reports**
- Replace lengthy status emails with a single page highlighting changes, blockers, and decisions needed. A micro-pivot is often simply a decision: "We'll drop Feature B and add Feature C next sprint because user feedback shows X." Having a short-form way to flag those changes accelerates action.
- **Dependency Stand-Ups**
- Hold weekly 15-minute cross-team meetings to surface interdependencies and mitigate risks early. In many large programs, the most expensive delays come from waiting on others. A short dependency stand-up is a micro-pivot enabler. When someone says,

"Team C is blocked by API delivery," that triggers an immediate micro-pivot (e.g., redirect Team C to a different task, escalate the API delay) rather than waiting until the monthly review.

- **Template Refreshes**
- Review project templates quarterly and update them based on user feedback. Templates often become stale and misaligned with current workflows. A small micro-pivot here, updating one form or board, can remove friction and improve adoption.
- **Risk Review Blitz**
- Schedule short, focused sessions (say 30 minutes) every two weeks to close out old risks and reprioritize emerging ones. Instead of treating risk review as a bi-annual exercise, make it a frequent rhythm. Each minor update is a micro-pivot.
- **Learning Moments**
- Encourage team members to share quick takeaways at the end of meetings, one insight, one improvement idea. These "micro-learning" actions build a habit of reflection and adjustment.

REAL-WORLD STARTUP EXAMPLES OF MICRO-PIVOTING

To illustrate micro-pivoting in action, let's draw from startup and agile examples where small shifts had big impacts.

Slack (origin: Tiny Speck → communication tool)

Slack began as a gaming company, Tiny Speck, building the game *Glitch*. When uptake failed, the team recognized that the internal communication tool they built for themselves was more valuable than the game. They made a pivot. While that is a macro-pivot, within that decision, they used micro-pivot patterns: they incrementally developed and rolled out their chat tool internally, iterated rapidly based on team feedback, and gradually shifted to market.

Key micro-pivot takeaways:

- They tested in production (their internal team) before full public rollout.
- They kept feature additions small and incremental.
- They responded to internal usage patterns rather than external speculation.

Agile Practices and Lean Startup

Eric Ries's *The Lean Startup* emphasizes small, structured experiments rather than large bets. Though Ries discusses "pivots," the approach aligns with micro-pivoting: build minimum viable products (MVPs), measure, learn, and iterate.

In agile leadership, as noted by the Scrum.org blog, leadership enables fast pivots by collecting real-time feedback, fostering collaboration, and enabling small iterations.

These methodologies underscore that micro-pivoting isn't just theory; it's embedded in how modern teams work.

The Micro-Pivot Concept in Other Domains

As highlighted in an article on micro-pivoting versus macro-pivoting, micro-pivots refer to mindset or strategy changes rather than major business transformations.

One piece, titled *Issue No. 56: The Power of Micro-Pivots,* emphasizes small shifts in strategy, product, messaging, or target audience driven by real-world feedback.HYPERLINK "https://nicolagraham.substack.com/p/issue-no56-the-power-of-micro-pivots?utm_source=chatgpt.com" \h These sources reinforce that micro-pivots are about minor, deliberate adjustments, not full-scale overhauls.

Micro-Pivots in Larger Organizations

Large organizations often struggle with inertia. Big change initiatives are expensive, risky, and slow. By contrast, micro-pivots provide a pathway to change that is incremental, manageable, and visible.

LEADERSHIP'S ROLE IN MICRO-PIVOTING

Micro-pivots don't happen on their own. They require leadership behaviors, not just processes.

- First, leaders must model adaptability. As Lee Iacocca said, "Apply yourself." In the context of micro-pivots, that means encouraging experimentation and rewarding initiative.
- Second, leaders must create safety for change. When a micro-pivot fails or yields no value, it's important that the team feels safe to learn. The leadership message should be: "Thank you for trying. What did we learn? How will we adjust?"
- Third, leaders must formalize micro-pivot mechanisms. Daily check-ins, lightweight status boards, and stop-and-learn retrospectives are rituals that require executive endorsement.
- Fourth, leaders must measure and communicate wins, however small. Recognizing small improvements reinforces the behavior. Over time,

the culture shifts toward constant refinement rather than "big bang" change.

PRACTICAL TIPS FOR IMPLEMENTING MICRO-PIVOTS

- **Start with low-risk changes**: Choose micro-pivots that won't jeopardize key deliverables but can provide visible improvement. For example, changing the format of a status meeting or swapping a report for a dashboard view.
- **Involve the team**: Micro-pivots should be bottom-up as much as top-down. Use retrospectives to ask, "What one thing would make your work easier this week?" Let the team surface potential pivots.
- **Track the impact**: Even micro-pivots should have a measurable outcome, less time spent in meetings, fewer blockers, and improved cadence. Tracking builds confidence and case studies for wider adoption.
- **Celebrate quick wins**: Share anecdotes in team meetings: "Because we changed our dependency stand-up cadence, Team X reduced hand-off delays by 40 % this sprint."
- **Document the learning**: A micro-pivot may be small, but its insight can benefit future teams. Capture what we tried, what happened, and what's next. Over time, this becomes a library of continuous improvement patterns.
- **Use tools to support the rhythm**: Lightweight tools like Kanban boards, decision logs, or dashboards help embed micro-pivoting. The

technology matters less than the habit of frequent, visible changes.

INTEGRATING AGILE METHODS AND MICRO-PIVOTS

Agile frameworks offer fertile ground for micro-pivots. Here are some specific practices:

- **Sprint Retrospectives**: At the end of each sprint, teams ask: "What one micro-pivot will we try next sprint to improve flow?"
- **Backlog Refinement**: Rather than a quarterly backlog overhaul, micro-pivot teams hold weekly refinement sessions to reprioritize based on the latest feedback.
- **Daily Stand-ups**: Use the classic three questions (What did I do? What will I do? What blocks me?) but add: "What small change will I make today to improve one thing?"
- **Kanban Flow Adjustments**: For teams using Kanban, a micro-pivot might be changing WIP limits mid-week, adjusting swimlanes, or moving from FIFO to priority-based pull.
- **Demo and Feedback Loops**: After each increment, teams solicit feedback from real users/customers and decide on one micro-pivot action for the next cycle.

By aligning agile rituals with micro-pivot behaviors, teams overcome the trap of "we'll improve later" and instead embed change into the rhythm of work.

STARTUP CASE STUDIES: MICRO-PIVOTING IN PRACTICE

Let's explore a few more startup-focused examples of how micro-pivots (or small, iterative shifts) have played a key role.

- **Instagram (then Burbn)**: Originally a complex location-based app, the founders observed that users most liked the photo-sharing component. Rather than scrap the product entirely, they made a **micro-pivot**: they stripped away most features, zeroed in on mobile photo sharing with filters, and rebranded as Instagram. While this looks like a macro-pivot, the real success came in the small, iterative steps: building a minimal version, releasing quickly, gathering user feedback, and adjusting repeatedly.
- **YouTube**: Started as a video-dating site, shifted to broader video-sharing. The pivot was driven by user behavior. The micro-pivot path is instructive: small but meaningful shifts in value proposition based on observed usage patterns.
- **Emerging Startups**: Articles on micro-pivoting vs macro-pivoting show that when organizations adopt frequent small changes, they build momentum and avoid considerable disruption.
- **Agile-led Startups**: A Scrum.org blog article highlights that startup agility, including the ability to pivot quickly, comes from leadership and culture, not just toolsets.

LEADERSHIP REFERENCES & FRAMEWORKS

To ground micro-pivots in leadership theory and behavior rather than just technique, consider these references:

- In *The Score Will Take Care of Itself*, Bill Walsh emphasizes precision, standards, and systems. Micro-pivots function like these systems: small, standardized adjustments embedded in daily routines that produce predictable results.
- In *Extreme Ownership*, Jocko Willink argues that leaders "own everything in their world." Micro-pivots are part of that ownership. Instead of waiting for higher-level change, teams and leaders take ownership of what they can change now.
- In *Trillion Dollar Coach*, Eric Schmidt recounts how Bill Campbell coached executives to have "the right conversations with the right people at the right time." Micro-pivots are precisely that: right conversations (retros, daily syncs) with right people (teams, dependencies) at the right time (weekly or daily).

Collectively, these leadership frameworks highlight that micro-pivots are not just process tweaks; they are leadership decisions embedded in culture, habits, and team mindset.

AVOIDING COMMON PITFALLS

While micro-pivots are powerful, they are not without risk. Here are some things to watch out for:

- **Over-tracking and analysis-paralysis**: If you treat every micro-pivot as a major review item, you lose the advantage of speed.
- **Change fatigue**: Although small, too many changes too quickly without rest can exhaust teams. Keep a sustainable cadence.
- **Lack of reflection**: If you make small changes but never reflect on whether they moved the needle, you're just changing for change's sake.
- **Cultural resistance**: Teams used to stable processes may resist frequent tweaks. Leadership must support psychological safety and clarify purpose.
- **Ignoring integration**: A small pivot in one team's workflow that misaligns with other teams can cause chaos. Always check cross-team impacts—even a slight shift needs context.

EMBEDDING MICRO-PIVOT RHYTHMS IN THE PROJECT ECONOMY

In a projectized world where teams form, deliver, and disband rapidly, micro-pivots offer a way to embed constant improvement without heavy coordination overhead. Here's how to embed the rhythm:

- **Cadence described explicitly**: Define when micro-pivot moments happen (end of day check-in, weekly stand-up, monthly review) and stick to it.
- **Visualize the backlog of improvements**: Maintain a simple board of "micro-pivot ideas" that the team can pull from.
- **Link to metrics**: Each micro-pivot should be tied to

a metric (e.g., reduce dependency wait time by 20%) to ensure outcome relevance.

- **Celebrate and share**: At project close-out or all-hands, spotlight micro-pivot winners: "Team Z tried the new template refresh—meeting prep time dropped by 15 %."
- **Scale the habit**: Over time, teach new teams micro-pivot practice, make it part of transfer-in onboarding for project teams.

CONCLUSION

Micro-pivots are the quiet drivers of sustainable success. By making small, measurable adjustments every day, teams build resilience and agility without the disruption of large-scale overhauls. As Covey reminds us, continuous renewal ensures long-term effectiveness. In a fast-changing project economy, the ability to pivot gracefully—one small step at a time is a decisive competitive advantage.

KEY TAKEAWAYS: MICRO-PIVOTS FOR EVERYDAY IMPACT

1. Small Changes Compound: Micro-pivots are not trivial adjustments; when practiced consistently, they create meaningful organizational shifts over time, just like compound interest.

2. Agility Lives in the Day-to-Day: High-velocity teams don't wait for annual restructures; they adapt through minor, continuous course corrections built into their daily rhythm.

3. Leadership Enables Micro-Pivots: Leaders set the tone by rewarding experimentation, modeling adaptability, and creating psychological safety for iterative change.

4. Startups Show the Way: Slack, Instagram, and YouTube demonstrate that micro-pivots—testing, learning, and refining quickly—can drive massive outcomes without massive disruption.

5. Agile Frameworks Reinforce the Practice: Scrum retrospectives, Kanban flow adjustments, daily stand-ups, and lean startup cycles are natural enablers of micro-pivoting.

6. Speed + Safety = Innovation: Small, low-risk changes allow teams to learn fast without derailing projects, making innovation a steady habit rather than a one-off event.

7. Document, Share, and Scale: Capturing micro-pivot learnings ensures they become part of the organization's muscle memory, enabling future teams to build on past wins.

8. Cultural Shift Over Structural Overhaul: Embedding micro-pivot rhythms shifts the culture toward continuous improvement without relying on expensive, high-disruption transformation programs.

9. Measure and Celebrate: Even the smallest pivots should have a visible impact. Recognizing and sharing these wins reinforces momentum and normalizes iterative improvement.

10. Micro-Pivots Are a Leadership Strategy: As leaders like Bill Walsh, Bill Campbell, and Jocko Willink have shown, disciplined systems, clear standards, and small, deliberate actions drive enduring success.

5

PROJECT MANAGEMENT TEMPLATE FORMS

Templates transform good intentions into repeatable practices. They provide structure, save time, and ensure that critical details are not overlooked. Below are practical, field-by-field guides to the core templates used by the NASA NAS Project Management Office (PMO). Each template is designed for easy adoption and can be adapted for organizations of any size.

1. Project Charter Template

Purpose: Establishes the project's vision, scope, and authority.

Key Fields:

- Project Name and ID: Unique identifier for tracking.
- Purpose/Problem Statement: One or two sentences explaining why the project exists.
- Objectives and Success Criteria: Measurable outcomes (e.g., "Reduce network latency by 20%").

- Scope Boundaries: What is included and excluded to prevent scope creep.
- Key Stakeholders and Roles: Sponsor, project manager, core team members.
- Milestones: High-level timeline with key decision points.
- Risks and Assumptions: Known uncertainties and conditions assumed to be true.

Usage Tip: Limit to one page for easy stakeholder review and approval.

2. Scope Statement & Work Breakdown Structure (WBS)

Purpose: Breaks down deliverables into manageable tasks.

Key Fields:

- Deliverables: List of products or services to be produced.
- Task Hierarchy: Parent tasks, sub-tasks, and work packages.
- Effort Estimates: Hours or days required for each work package.
- Resource Assignments: Names or roles responsible for each task.

Usage Tip: Use spreadsheet software or project management tools to maintain clarity as tasks evolve.

3. Communication Plan

Purpose: Defines how information flows among stakeholders.

Key Fields:

- Audience: Executives, team members, external partners.
- Message Type: Status updates, risk alerts, decision requests.
- Frequency: Daily stand-ups, weekly summaries, monthly reviews.
- Channel: Email, chat, dashboards, or in-person meetings.

Usage Tip: Link to the project charter to maintain consistency in messaging.

4. Schedule Template

Purpose: Provides a detailed plan for task sequencing and timing.

Key Fields:

- Task Name: Descriptive label for each activity.
- Start and Finish Dates: Planned timeline for each task.
- Dependencies: Predecessor tasks that must finish before the next begins.
- Critical Path Indicator: Highlights tasks that determine overall project duration.
- Buffer Time: Built-in contingency for high-risk activities.

Usage Tip: Combine with a Gantt chart for visual tracking.

5. Risk Register

Purpose: Tracks potential events that could impact project objectives.

Key Fields:

- Risk Description: Clear statement of the uncertainty.
- Probability (High/Medium/Low): Likelihood of occurrence.
- Impact (High/Medium/Low): Potential effect on scope, schedule, or cost.
- Mitigation Strategy: Planned actions to reduce probability or impact.
- Owner: Person responsible for monitoring and mitigating the risk.

Usage Tip: Review and update weekly to maintain relevance.

6. Decision Log

Purpose: Records key decisions and their rationale.

Key Fields:

- Decision Date: When the decision was made.
- Decision Summary: Brief description of the choice.
- Options Considered: Alternatives evaluated.
- Responsible Parties: Individuals who made or approved the decision.

Usage Tip: Keep concise but complete; decisions are invaluable during audits or retrospectives.

7. Change Request Form

Purpose: Formalizes proposed modifications to scope, schedule, or resources.

Key Fields:

- Change Description: What is changing and why.
- Impact Assessment: Effect on cost, schedule, and risk.
- Approval Section: Sign-offs from sponsor and PMO lead.

Usage Tip: Pair with the Change Control Board process to ensure timely review.

8. One-Page Status Report

Purpose: Provides a snapshot of project health for busy stakeholders.

Key Fields:

- Current Phase: Initiation, planning, execution, or closure.
- Recent Accomplishments: Highlights since the last report.
- Upcoming Milestones: Key events in the next reporting period.
- Risks/Issues: Top concerns requiring attention.
- Decisions Needed: Actions required from leadership.

Usage Tip: Use visuals such as traffic-light indicators (green/yellow/red) for quick comprehension.

9. Lessons Learned Canvas

Purpose: Captures insights into future projects.

Key Fields:

- Successes: What went well and why.
- Challenges: Obstacles encountered and how they were addressed.
- Recommendations: Suggestions for improving future projects.
- Action Items: Specific steps to implement improvements.

Usage Tip: Conduct a team workshop at project close-out to complete the canvas collaboratively.

IMPLEMENTATION TIPS

- Start Simple: Introduce one or two templates at a time to avoid overwhelming teams.
- Customize Thoughtfully: Adapt templates to your organization's needs without diluting essential fields.
- Store in a Shared Repository: Use a version-controlled platform to ensure everyone accesses the latest template.
- Train and Reinforce: Provide quick reference guides and coaching to promote consistent use.

Templates are more than administrative tools—they are enablers of clarity, accountability, and continuous improvement. As Lee Iacocca would say, "The discipline of writing something down is the first step toward making it happen." By adopting these forms and tailoring them to your environment, you create a foundation for repeatable success across projects of any size.

PART SIX
FINAL THOUGHTS

1

PROJECTIZED WORK AND THE AMERICAN FAMILY
AWARENESS AND ACTION

GENERATIONAL CYCLES AND THE PROJECT PARADIGM

Neil Howe, in *The Fourth Turning*, describes history as unfolding in recurring generational cycles—growth, unraveling, crisis, and renewal. Each "turning" shapes the values, institutions, and work patterns of the society that lives through it. The United States, according to Howe, is entering a Fourth Turning: an era of turbulence that demands new structures of trust, responsibility, and adaptation.

Projectization can be viewed as both a symptom and a solution within this cycle. As traditional institutions—corporations, governments, and long-term employment—lose stability, individuals and families are being pushed to self-organize around short, mission-based commitments. This mirrors the historical pattern Howe describes: when large systems weaken, smaller, purpose-driven units—families, communities, and teams—become the engines of renewal.

The project economy, then, is not merely a business trend; it is a societal adaptation to cyclical change. Just as previous generations rebuilt after crisis moments such as the Great Depression or World War II, today's professionals and families are constructing new frameworks of meaning and cooperation. *The Fourth Turning* warns that every cycle ends in reconstruction; *Project Paradigm* offers a blueprint for rebuilding—one project, one team, and one household at a time.

Quote Highlight: "History is seasonal, and winter is coming. But the cold can bring clarity, renewal, and strength." Neil Howe, *The Fourth Turning*.

THE HUMAN DIMENSION OF PROJECTIZATION

The rise of project-based employment offers freedom and flexibility, but it also tests the foundations of the American family. In a contract-driven economy, careers unfold as portfolios of short missions—each with its own rhythm, income stream, and demands. This shift empowers individuals to design work around purpose and autonomy, yet it also introduces volatility that families must learn to navigate with foresight and discipline.

ECONOMIC RIPPLES

In a projectized world, stability gives way to variability. Income ebbs and flows with contract cycles; benefits once guaranteed by employers now require personal management. For dual-income families, this model can foster creativity and shared resilience. For single-income households, it can magnify financial strain and uncertainty. Rising costs in housing, childcare, and education make financial literacy and proactive planning indispensable life skills. Projectization thus transforms not only how people work, but how they save, spend, and plan for the future.

HEALTH INSURANCE AND FAMILY STABILITY

Perhaps the most profound economic consequence of projectized work is the erosion of employer-based health coverage. In the traditional model, families relied on company plans for affordable, stable care. In the project economy, that safety net often disappears. Families must now secure their own policies, manage fluctuating premiums, and navigate complex coverage options.

This burden affects more than finances—it shapes family decisions about where to live, when to have children, and whether to take entrepreneurial risks. Jordan Peterson reminds us that meaning arises through responsibility; in this context, families must assume new responsibility for their own health and stability. Practical strategies include:

- Maintaining a robust emergency fund for medical costs.
- Exploring professional associations or group insurance pools.
- Treating health coverage as an annual "family project," reviewed with the same rigor as a budget.
- Advocating for policy reforms that decouple healthcare from traditional employment.

Families that face this challenge consciously through planning, savings, and shared accountability can transform vulnerability into resilience.

CULTURAL SHIFTS AND PSYCHOLOGICAL ANCHORS

As Jordan Peterson argues in *12 Rules for Life*, meaningful work and stable family structures are the bedrock of psychological well-being. The danger of a purely gig-based existence lies in its transience; if every project is treated as disposable, people may lose the deeper sense of purpose that comes from enduring commitments. However, projectization also holds opportunity. It allows families to align work with values, choose projects that reflect their priorities, and design rhythms that balance productivity and presence. The key lies in intentional structure—building stability through habits rather than institutions.

PRACTICAL PATTERNS FOR FAMILY ADAPTATION

- Shared Calendars and Portfolio Reviews: Weekly family check-ins align project deadlines with school, caregiving, and community life.
- Financial Buffers: Larger emergency reserves smooth gaps between contracts and provide emotional security.
- Health Security Planning: Treat insurance and preventive care as ongoing, shared responsibilities.
- Meaningful Metrics: Evaluate work not only by income but by alignment with family values.
- Rituals of Continuity: Daily meals, bedtime

routines, and weekend traditions ground families amid changing workloads.

The projectized family thrives not by eliminating uncertainty, but by mastering it.

Awareness → Action

The Project Paradigm is not merely a framework for managing work—it's a mindset for living intentionally in a dynamic world. Awareness of change is not enough; action must follow. As Stephen Covey teaches, we must "Begin with the End in Mind." Awareness illuminates the path, but discipline and purpose turn vision into movement.

KEY TAKEAWAYS

1. Projectization Is Here to Stay: From startups to federal agencies, project-based work is the new default structure of productivity.

2. Strong Foundations Endure: Charters, communication plans, and risk registers provide the scaffolding that supports both projects and families.

3. Culture Over Control: Transparency, trust, and communication matter more than hierarchy.

4. Technology Amplifies Humanity: AI and automation extend human reach—but leadership, empathy, and ethics remain non-automatable.

5. Continuous Improvement Sustains Success: Micro-pivots and lessons learned apply not only to teams, but to households and communities.

MOVING FROM AWARENESS TO ACTION

Awareness is understanding that work and life have changed; action is building systems that thrive within that reality.

- Draft a charter for your next family or professional project—define purpose, scope, and success metrics.
- Establish a rhythm of one-page updates or weekly reflections to maintain clarity.
- Identify one micro-pivot you can implement this week—at work or at home.
- Explore automation tools that remove administrative clutter and free time for connection.

James Altucher's challenge to "become an idea machine" applies here: generate ideas for improving both work and home systems. Most will be small; a few will be transformative.

A CALL TO LEADERS AND FAMILIES

Whether leading a team, a household, or both, the charge is the same: create environments where people can succeed and grow. Leadership today means balancing flexibility with structure, freedom with responsibility, and short-term wins with long-term purpose. As Lee Iacocca wrote, "The ability to concentrate and to use your time well is everything." That truth applies equally to the boardroom and the dinner table.

FINAL REFLECTION

The project economy is not a threat to the American family— it is a call to redesign it with intention. By integrating structure, communication, and shared responsibility, families can transform uncertainty into opportunity. As this book has shown, the same principles that guide successful projects—clarity of purpose, disciplined communication, and continuous learning—also sustain successful lives.

The future belongs to those who turn awareness into action, one project, one habit, and one conversation at a time. The Project Paradigm is not a destination. It is a way of seeing—of building stability through motion, and meaning through mindful work.

NOTES
THE SHIFT

CHAPTER 1: THE PROJECT-BASED ECONOMY

CORE IDEA

Work is moving from permanent roles to projects as the primary unit of value delivery.

Organizations now thrive on missions—purposeful, time-bound efforts—rather than static positions.

This shift demands adaptability from both individuals and organizations.

1. From Jobs to Missions

- Traditional careers (20th century): stability, fixed roles, hierarchical ladders.
- Modern economy: bounded missions with measurable outcomes and cross-functional teams.
- Guy Standing (2011) warns of *The Precariat*, a class facing insecurity from short-term work.

- Opportunity: become a "project entrepreneur"—adaptable, skilled, and self-directed.
- Stephen Covey (1989): "Be Proactive" and "Begin with the End in Mind" → project charter mindset.

2. Why Projects Are Winning

(a) Coordination Costs Have Collapsed

- Digital and AI tools (Teams, Slack, Zoom, Asana) make remote alignment nearly frictionless.
- Lee Iacocca (2007): challenges create hidden opportunities; collaboration is now instantaneous.

(b) Volatility Rewards Agility

- Projects allow rapid pivots as markets and technologies evolve.
- Iacocca's "fast action teams" exemplify agility and time discipline.

(c) Talent Wants Flexibility

- Millennials/Gen Z value autonomy, skill variety, and purpose over hierarchy.
- James Altucher (2013) "Choose Yourself" era: create your own opportunities.

(d) Economics Favor Variable Capacity

- Firms shift from fixed payrolls to project-based funding.

- Kogon & Blakemore (2015): even informal teams
  need PM discipline: scope, stakeholders,
  communication.

3. Career Implications: Résumé → Portfolio

- Success narrative is now framed by projects delivered
  and value created.
- Replace "5 years at Company X" with impact
  statements:
- *e.g., "Led a project that reduced processing time by
  40%."*
- Each project becomes a leadership case study.
- Altucher's "idea machine" principle → continuous
  creativity and experimentation.
- Everyone is an unofficial project manager (Kogon &
  Blakemore).

4. Organizational Implications: Value Flows Through Portfolios

- Leaders must manage portfolios, not departments.
- Metrics that matter: throughput, forecast accuracy,
  stakeholder satisfaction.
- Iacocca's Chrysler turnaround: project portfolio
  discipline during crisis.
- Modern PMOs = lightweight governance hubs,
  enabling transparency and accountability.

5. The Human Side of the Shift

- Standing's "precariat" highlights emotional and economic risks: instability, anxiety.
- Covey's "Sharpen the Saw" → renewal and resilience are essential.
- Individuals: build savings, networks, and lifelong learning habits.
- Organizations: provide portable benefits, knowledge continuity, and psychological safety.
- "People drive projects, not processes." *Kogon & Blakemore.*

6. NASA as a Living Example

- NAS Division at NASA Ames embodies projectization:
  - Temporary, cross-disciplinary teams deliver HPC upgrades, GPU integrations, and data migrations.
  - Predictability, speed, and measurable progress prioritized.
- Reflects the shift from operations to mission-based collaboration.

7. Action Takeaways

For Individuals

- Think in missions—treat every role as a project.
- Capture metrics, milestones, and stories from each effort.

- Strengthen adaptability, communication, and risk
  management.

For Organizations

- Fund outcomes, not departments.
- Enable internal talent marketplaces.
- Track metrics that indicate value flow—not just
  effort spent.

8. Key Themes

Theme	Summary
Nature of Work	Permanent jobs → project-based missions
Individual Focus	Portfolio careers; adaptability as an advantage
Organizational Focus	Portfolios and lean PMOs drive value
Technology	Collaboration tools collapse coordination time
Human Factor	Stability traded for autonomy and upskilling
Leadership	Vision translated into executable missions

9. Memorable Quotes

- "Be Proactive." —Stephen Covey
- "We are continually faced with great opportunities brilliantly disguised as insoluble problems." —Lee Iacocca
- "No one is going to pick you." —James Altucher
- "People drive projects, not processes." —Kogon & Blakemore
- "Good business leaders create a vision, articulate the vision, passionately own the vision, and relentlessly drive it to completion." —Jack Welch

CHAPTER 2: WHY NOW? TECHNOLOGY, ECONOMICS, AND DEMOGRAPHICS

CORE IDEA

The rise of the project-based economy is no coincidence—it is the result of three converging forces: Technology, Economics, and Demographics.

Each reinforces the others, creating a self-accelerating cycle that rewards agility, speed, and purpose-driven leadership.

1. Technology: Acceleration Without Borders

- Cloud computing (Azure, AWS, Google Cloud) has made infrastructure on demand—minutes, not months.
- Collaboration tools (Zoom, Slack, Trello) remove geographic barriers; distributed teams act in real time.
- Artificial intelligence reduces administrative

overhead—meeting summaries, risk detection, and task automation.
- Lee Iacocca: "*The speed of communication is the speed of business.*"
  - In today's digital landscape, that speed is effectively instantaneous.
- Result: forming, launching, and executing projects globally is now feasible, fast, and efficient.

2. Economics: Volatility Favors Flexibility

- Market instability rewards variable capacity—scaling resources up or down quickly.
- Project contracts replace fixed payrolls, allowing rapid response to demand cycles.
- Guy Standing's *Precariat* warns of instability for workers, but flexibility is also a competitive weapon.
- Leaders must "begin with the end in mind" (Covey): sustainability, not just cost reduction.
- James Altucher (2013): advocates diversified income and self-created opportunity.
  - Economic uncertainty becomes an opportunity when individuals "own their runway."

3. Demographics: A Workforce That Demands Meaning and Mobility

- Millennials + Gen Z = majority of the workforce.
- These generations prioritize purpose, autonomy, and growth over permanence.
- Kogon & Blakemore (2015): project work fits their ethos: clear goals, deadlines, and visible results.

- Digital natives expect anywhere/anytime collaboration—seamless integration with project models.
- Career progression is redefined as a portfolio of achievements, not a climb up a ladder.

4. The Intersection: Technology + Economics + Demographics

- These forces interlock:
    - Technology enables flexible work.
    - Economic volatility rewards agility.
    - Demographic expectations normalize project-based employment.
- Peter Drucker: *"The best way to predict the future is to create it."*
- Leadership imperative: make it happen—design, adapt, and lead within the convergence.

5. Risks and Safeguards

Risks

- Income variability and burnout.
- Rapid turnover → erosion of institutional knowledge.

Safeguards

- Individuals:
    - Apply Covey's "Sharpen the Saw": constant renewal, health, and skill development.

- Altucher's "idea machine" method: generate and test new ideas continually.
  - Organizations:
    - Use lightweight governance: charters, comms plans, risk registers.
    - Balance flexibility with accountability—enable agility without chaos.
  - NASA NAS Division — demonstrates this equilibrium:
    - PMO templates and structured reviews enable visibility, risk control, and speed in parallel.

6. Conclusion

Technology removes barriers.

Economics rewards agility.

Demographics demand purpose.

- The project-based economy is not a trend but a structural transformation in how value is created.

Lee Iacocca: *"In times of great change, you can either lead, follow, or get out of the way."*

Leadership today means choosing to lead by creating purpose and improving execution.

7. Key Themes

Theme	Summary
Technology	Collapsed coordination costs enable instant collaboration.
Economics	Volatility favors scalable, project-based capacity.
Demographics	New generations seek purpose and mobility.
Leadership	Must harness convergence, not resist it.
Safeguards	Lightweight governance and lifelong learning sustain agility.
Cultural Shift	The project mindset replaces the career ladder with the mission portfolio.

8. Memorable Quotes

- "The speed of communication is the speed of business." —Lee Iacocca
- "Begin with the end in mind." —Stephen Covey
- "Own your own runway." —James Altucher
- "The best way to predict the future is to create it." —Peter Drucker
- "Change before you have to." —Jack Welch

CHAPTER 3: EVIDENCE OF THE SHIFT

CORE IDEA

The project-based economy is no longer theoretical; it's quantifiable, observable, and accelerating.

From freelance markets and technology platforms to internal enterprise transformations, measurable data and real-world behaviors confirm that projects have become the dominant mode of value delivery.

1. Labor Market Signals

- Freelance platforms (Upwork, Toptal, Fiverr) report record revenues and expanding talent pools annually.
- Contract and independent work have grown several times faster than traditional employment.
- Guy Standing's *The Precariat* warns that this rise reshapes job security and identity, yet it also empowers flexibility.

- Fortune 500 enterprises now host internal gig marketplaces, letting employees bid for short-term projects.
  - Workers "choose themselves" (*Altucher*) within organizations, self-directing toward meaningful work.
- Labor markets increasingly value adaptability, mission-completion, and portfolio-based experience over tenure.

2. Technology Adoption Metrics

- Tools like Jira, Asana, Smartsheet, Monday.com, and Trello show double-digit annual growth.
- These platforms serve as the digital backbone of projectized work—enabling visibility, collaboration, and accountability.
- AI integration further enhances productivity:
  - Predicting schedule risks
  - Allocating resources dynamically
  - Drafting risk assessments and summaries
- Stephen Covey's "Put First Things First": technology enables focus on high-value activities by automating the rest.
- The result: technology has become the operating system of the project economy.

3. Organizational Case Studies

- NASA's Advanced Supercomputing (NAS) Division:
  - Transitioned from operations-centric to project-centric workflows.

- Established a PMO with charters, review cadences, and performance metrics.
  - Outcomes: reduced cycle times, improved forecasting, stronger accountability culture.
- Lee Iacocca's Chrysler turnaround—an early precursor of modern projectization:
  - Defined initiatives, milestones, and accountability-driven leadership.
- Other sectors mirror the same trend:
  - Finance → regulatory compliance projects
  - Healthcare → telemedicine deployment
  - Public Sector → smart-city modernization projects
- Common pattern: replacing static roles with dynamic, outcome-driven charters.

4. Cultural Evidence

- Vocabulary of work is changing: gig, sprint, deliverable, velocity, backlog.
- Professionals describe themselves by projects delivered, not job titles held.
- Kory Kogon & Suzette Blakemore: everyone is an unofficial project manager, regardless of role.
- James Altucher: encourages building a "public trail" —talks, code, templates, publications—that form a visible project portfolio.
- Career reputation now depends on contribution visibility and cross-domain adaptability.

5. Implications and Meaning

- For Individuals:
    - Develop portable skills: communication, planning, stakeholder management.
    - Apply Covey's "Seek First to Understand" when integrating into new teams and contexts.
    - Treat every project as a learning investment and proof of adaptability.
- For Organizations:
    - Embrace internal marketplaces and outcome-based rewards.
    - Foster lightweight governance (charters, comms plans, risk registers).
    - Abandon "yesterday's logic" (*Peter Drucker*): design for agility, not permanence.
- The future belongs to organizations that design for adaptability, not stability.

6. Conclusion

Across metrics, technologies, and mindsets, the Project Paradigm is visible and measurable.

The debate is over; the pace of adaptation now determines success.

Lee Iacocca: *"Even a correct decision is wrong when it is taken too late."*

- The moment for transformation isn't in the future—it's now.

7. Key Themes

Theme	Summary
Labor Market	Freelance and contract work outpacing full-time jobs; internal gig models rising.
Technology	Collaboration and AI tools serve as the "OS" for projectized work.
Organizational Change	Project structures improve agility, cycle time, and accountability.
Cultural Shift	Work language and identity defined by projects, not titles.
Individual Adaptation	Portfolio careers and continuous learning as survival tools.
Leadership Imperative	Avoid "yesterday's logic" — design for mobility and adaptability.

8. Memorable Quotes

- "Choose yourself." —James Altucher
- "Put First Things First." —Stephen Covey
- "The greatest danger in times of turbulence is not the turbulence; it is to act with yesterday's logic." —Peter Drucker
- "Even a correct decision is wrong when it is taken too late." —Lee Iacocca
- "Everyone is an unofficial project manager." — Kogon & Blakemor

NOTES

CORE KNOWLEDGE FOR
A PROJECTIZED WORLD

CHAPTER 4: FRAMEWORKS: AGILE, WATERFALL, AND HYBRID TAILORING

CORE IDEA

The transition to project-based work requires more than new mindsets—it demands the right frameworks to deliver predictable results in unpredictable environments.

Agile, Waterfall, and Hybrid approaches provide a toolbox of methods for structuring, adapting, and tailoring execution. The effective leader selects and evolves the framework to fit the mission, not the other way around.

1. No Silver Bullet

- There is no single "best" methodology—only contextually appropriate tools.
- Framework choice must begin with clarity:
  - Desired outcomes
  - Degree of uncertainty
  - Regulatory and stakeholder requirements
- Henry Ford: "Don't find fault, find a remedy."

- Stephen Covey: "Begin with the end in mind."—
  choose frameworks based on purpose, not
  popularity.
- The goal is fit-for-purpose project design, not
  methodological perfection.

2. Agile: Embracing Change

- Originated in software, now adopted across
  marketing, education, research, and government.
- Core values:
  - Individuals & interactions over processes &
    tools
  - Working solutions over documentation
  - Responding to change rather than following
    a plan
- Scrum, Kanban, Lean Startup = dominant Agile
  variants.
- Strengths: short cycles, continuous feedback, and
  visible progress.

Alignment with Thinkers

- James Altucher: "Choose yourself" →
  empowerment through self-organized teams.
- Kogon & Blakemore: "Unofficial PMs" thrive in
  Agile because leadership is distributed.
- Tuckman's Team Development Model:
  - *Forming:* Orientation & trust-building.
  - *Storming:* Conflict & clarity through feedback.
  - *Norming:* Established rhythms and norms.
  - *Performing:* High velocity, minimal friction.
  - *Adjourning:* Reflection and lessons learned.

- Agile teams evolve like living systems—growing through feedback and trust.
- Requires a culture of psychological safety, lightweight governance, and empowerment.

3. Waterfall: The Power of Predictability

- Sequential, phase-based model: Requirements → Design → Build → Test → Deploy.
- Emphasizes planning, documentation, and formal sign-offs.
- Best for projects with:
  - Stable requirements
  - High compliance needs
  - Safety or mission-critical stakes (e.g., aerospace, healthcare, infrastructure)
- Lee Iacocca's Chrysler turnaround exemplified disciplined, phase-based execution.
- NASA's infrastructure and supercomputing projects often employ Waterfall rigor for assurance and accountability.
- Advantage: clarity, traceability, and risk control.

4. Hybrid: The Best of Both Worlds

- Most organizations now use Hybrid approaches:
  - Waterfall discipline upfront (scope, security, risk, cost)
  - Agile iteration for design, testing, and innovation
- Covey's "Synergize"—blending strengths to achieve superior outcomes.
- Hybrid frameworks allow structure without sacrificing adaptability.

- Common example: NASA NAS—formal charters + Agile sprints for research and development.
- Reflects Iacocca's principle: *"Apply yourself, get the facts, then act decisively."*

5. Tailoring the Framework

Frameworks evolve as conditions change—tailoring is a dynamic, ongoing process.

Practical Tailoring Checklist:

- Uncertainty: How stable are requirements?
- Compliance: Are there safety or regulatory constraints?
- Integration Complexity: How many systems/teams must align?
- Stakeholder Cadence: How often do sponsors need updates or demos?
- Delivery Risk: What is the cost of delay or failure?
- Team Maturity: How familiar are members with Agile or Waterfall?

James Altucher's "micro-pivots" reflect this mindset: Make small, frequent adjustments to maintain alignment without major disruption.

Kory Kogon: Leaders must regularly ask, *"Does our current method still serve the outcome?"*

6. Cultural Considerations

- Framework success depends on organizational culture.
- Resistance arises when methods are imposed without context or dialogue.
- Stephen Covey: *"Seek first to understand, then to be understood."*
- Effective leaders engage teams in why a framework is used and how it benefits them.
- Trust, transparency, and open communication enable authentic adoption rather than forced compliance.

7. Conclusion

Frameworks are means to an end, not ideologies.

- Agile delivers adaptability and speed.
- Waterfall provides rigor and predictability.
- Hybrid balances both through intelligent tailoring.
- The skilled project leader blends structure and flexibility—applying judgment, not dogma.

Lee Iacocca: *"The ability to concentrate and to use your time well is everything."*

The proper framework channels that focus on measurable progress and sustained momentum.

8. Key Themes

Theme	Summary
Framework Fit	Frameworks are tools, not dogmas; select based on context.
Agile Strength	Adaptability, feedback, and empowerment for dynamic environments.
Waterfall Strength	Predictability and control for regulated or high-risk projects.
Hybrid Advantage	Combines adaptability with governance for balanced performance.
Tailoring Principle	Continuous refinement through "micro-pivots" and reflection.
Culture First	Frameworks fail without trust, dialogue, and understanding.
Leadership Focus	Clear vision, decisive execution, and disciplined concentration ensure success.

9. Memorable Quotes

- "Don't find fault, find a remedy." —Henry Ford
- "Begin with the end in mind." —Stephen Covey
- "Choose yourself." —James Altucher
- "Apply yourself, get the facts, then act decisively." —Lee Iacocca
- "Seek first to understand, then to be understood." —Stephen Covey
- "Good business leaders create a vision . . . and relentlessly drive it to completion." —Jack Welch

CHAPTER 5: THE CHARTER—VISION, SCOPE, AND ALIGNMENT

CORE IDEA

If a project is a journey, the charter is both map and compass —defining purpose, success, and boundaries.

Projects rarely fail in execution; they fail in initiation, when purpose and scope lack clarity.

The charter transforms intent into alignment, converting vision into coordinated action.

1. Why a Charter Matters

- Peter Drucker: *"Plans are only good intentions unless they immediately degenerate into hard work."*
  - The charter is that moment of degeneration— where ideas become commitments.
- Serves as a contract of understanding between sponsors, teams, and stakeholders.

- Converts a vision into actionable direction, establishing alignment and accountability.
- Stephen Covey's *"Begin with the End in Mind"* is embodied here—clarity before execution.

Core Elements of a Charter

- Vision & Problem Statement: Why the project exists and what need it addresses.
- Objectives & Success Criteria: Measurable outcomes that define completion.
- Scope Boundaries & Deliverables: What's in and what's out.
- Stakeholders & Roles: Ownership, sponsorship, and accountability.
- Milestones & Risks: Key checkpoints and known uncertainties.

2. Building the Charter Collaboratively

- Kory Kogon & Suzette Blakemore: co-creation builds trust and shared ownership.
- Early collaboration surfaces assumptions before they become friction points.
- James Altucher's "idea machine" metaphor—everyone contributes insights and risks.
- Outcome → a shared mental model of success, not a bureaucratic formality.

3. Practical Steps to Draft a Charter

i. Frame the Why: Concise problem statement + inspirational vision.
ii. Define Success: Quantify results. Lee Iacocca: *"Decisions without numbers are just conversations."*
iii. Set Boundaries: Clarify exclusions to control scope.
iv. Identify Stakeholders: Define influence, funding, and authority lines.
v. Outline Milestones: Show time-based decision gates.
vi. List Risks & Assumptions: Expose uncertainties early.

4. NASA NAS Example

- NAS's standardized Project Charter Template governs all major initiatives—GPU clusters, data upgrades, security improvements.
- Each charter clarifies objectives, resources, and risks before launch.
- Benefits: faster approvals, fewer mid-project surprises, improved portfolio visibility.
- Demonstrates how discipline at initiation yields agility later.

5. Living Document, Not Static Artifact

- The charter must evolve with the project.
- Revisit at milestones to validate scope, risk, and stakeholder alignment.
- Covey's "Put First Things First"—daily actions should mirror the charter's priorities.

- A "living charter" sustains focus and integrity as conditions change.

6. Communicating the Charter

- Hidden charters = useless charters.
- Simplify into one-page visuals or infographics highlighting: purpose, scope, milestones, ownership.
- Henry Gantt: *"The real value of any plan is not merely its creation, but its communication and execution."*
- Embed a communication plan directly in the charter:
  - Who receives updates
  - Frequency & format
  - Decision escalation paths
- Visibility = power: clarity must be constant, not episodic.

7. Strategic Value of Clarity

- In fast-moving environments, charters are stabilizing anchors.
- Provide boundaries for decision-making, enabling speed without chaos.
- At portfolio level:
  - Support smarter prioritization
  - Ensure objective resource allocation
  - Enable consistent progress tracking
- The charter becomes "the currency of clarity"—linking speed, adaptability, and accountability.

8. Conclusion

A strong charter defines the why, the what, and the how before any resource is committed.

It aligns people, expectations, and outcomes—turning abstract ideas into executable missions.

In the project economy, where teams assemble and disband rapidly, the charter is a north star ensuring coherence amid change.

Leaders who invest in clarity upfront minimize confusion downstream and accelerate delivery.

Lee Iacocca: *"The ability to concentrate and to use your time well is everything."*

A precise charter directs that concentration toward purposeful results

9. Key Themes

Theme	Summary
Foundation of Success	Most project failures originate in unclear charters.
Alignment Through Clarity	Vision + scope + success criteria = shared understanding.
Collaborative Creation	Co-authorship builds trust and accountability.
Communication	Visibility and simplicity give the charter power.
Living Governance	Revisited and updated — not filed and forgotten.
Strategic Advantage	Enables agility with accountability; guides portfolio decisions.
Leadership Discipline	Clarity and focus turn intention into measurable impact.

10. Memorable Quotes

- "Plans are only good intentions unless they immediately degenerate into hard work." —Peter Drucker
- "Begin with the End in Mind." —Stephen Covey
- "Decisions without numbers are just conversations." —Lee Iacocca
- "The real value of any plan is not merely its creation, but its communication and execution." —Henry Gantt
- "Seek First to Understand." —Stephen Covey

CHAPTER 6:
COMMUNICATION AS
THE OPERATING SYSTEM

CORE IDEA

Projects don't fail because of Gantt charts—they fail because of silence, ambiguity, or misalignment.

Communication is the operating system that keeps all other project components running.

In a distributed, fast-moving, project-based economy, clarity and cadence are what separate chaos from cohesion.

1. Why Communication Matters

- Stephen Covey: "*Seek first to understand, then to be understood.*"—Empathetic listening precedes influence.
- Peter Drucker: "*The most important thing in communication is hearing what isn't said.*"—Great leaders detect the unspoken risks beneath updates.

- Bill Walsh: Communication standards are leadership standards. Calm, consistent clarity under pressure sets the emotional tone for the team.
- Henry Gantt: *"A man doing his best always becomes better."*—Clear expectations empower continuous improvement.
- Lee Iacocca: *"You can have brilliant ideas, but if you can't get them across, your ideas won't get you anywhere."*
  - Communication translates ideas into coordinated action.

Core Principle:

Projects succeed when leaders listen deeply, communicate clearly, and create predictable rhythms for information flow.

2. Communication as a System, Not a Side Task

- Communication integrates scope, schedule, risk, and cost into a single, living framework.
- Like a computer's OS, it manages inputs (updates), processes (decisions), and outputs (actions).
- Effective communication synchronizes distributed teams, ensuring alignment amid volatility.

3. Elements of a Communication Plan

A structured plan answers four questions:

- Who needs to know what?
- How often must they be informed?

- Through which channels (email, meetings, dashboards, chat)?
- What actions or decisions should follow?

Best Practice—Kogon & Blakemore:

Keep the plan one page, linked directly to the project charter.

Include feedback loops.

Communication is a dialogue, not a broadcast.

Example: NASA NAS PMO meetings always reserve Q&A time to surface risks and dependencies.

4. Making Status Useful

Poor updates report activity; effective ones report progress and change.

High-Value Status Reports Highlight:

- Deltas: What has changed since the last update?
- Risks & Blockers: Threats to schedule or quality.
- Decisions Needed: Clear asks for leaders.

James Altucher: *"Over-communicate clarity."*

- Brevity, visuals, and relevance show respect for time and sharpen understanding.

Use dashboards and one-page summaries to emphasize movement, not motion.

5. Building Trust Through Transparency

- Projects accelerate when issues surface early.
- Covey's "Emotional Bank Account": every honest update is a deposit; silence or surprise is a withdrawal.
- Bill Walsh: *"Champions behave like champions before they're champions."*
  - Model honesty and accountability from the top.
- Share bad news early, paired with solution options—this creates credibility and momentum.

6. Technology as a Communication Multiplier

- Tools amplify communication speed but can also create noise.
- Balance real-time (Slack, Teams) and asynchronous (dashboards, weekly briefs) channels.
- Bill Walsh's "standard of clarity": every message must align, direct, or inspire.
- Lee Iacocca: warned against mistaking activity for progress.
  - Choose the *fewest* effective channels that reach the *widest* audience with the *highest* clarity.

7. NASA Case Example

At NASA's Advanced Supercomputing Division (NAS):

- Weekly dependency stand-ups maintain cross-team visibility.
- Monthly portfolio reviews align strategic direction.

- The PMO one-page status template tracks:
  - Deltas (change since last update)
  - Blockers (risks)
  - Required decisions (for leadership). This delivers transparency without overload.

8. Practical Tips for Communication Excellence

- Begin every meeting by stating the decision or outcome sought.
- Use visuals to explain dependencies.
- Encourage open debate → then "disagree and commit."
- Capture and distribute actions and owners within 24 hours.
- Reinforce clarity standards through repetition and visible follow-through.

9. Conclusion

Communication is the invisible infrastructure of every project.

Plans fail when communication falters; success follows cultures that prize clarity, trust, and rhythm.

Lee Iacocca: *"The ability to get along with people is as important as being technically competent."*

Bill Walsh proved that when communication standards are high, *"the score takes care of itself."*

In a project economy where teams form and dissolve rapidly, communication mastery is the core competency that sustains every other metric.

10. Key Themes

Theme	Summary
Communication as OS	The foundation connecting scope, schedule, cost, and risk.
Listening First	Empathy uncovers hidden risks and builds trust.
Clarity = Velocity	Clear, concise messages turn vision into execution.
Structured Plans	Define audiences, cadence, channels, and decisions.
Transparency = Speed	Early honesty accelerates problem-solving.
Tech Discipline	Fewer channels; greater purpose and clarity.
Leadership Through Voice	Calm, precise communication sets team culture.

11. Memorable Quotes

- "Seek first to understand, then to be understood." —Stephen Covey
- "The most important thing in communication is hearing what isn't said." —Peter Drucker
- "You can have brilliant ideas, but if you can't get them across, your ideas won't get you anywhere." —Lee Iacocca
- "Champions behave like champions before they're champions." —Bill Walsh
- "A man doing his best always becomes better." —Henry Gantt

- "The ability to get along with people is as important as being technically competent." —Lee Iacocca

NOTES

CASEWORK FROM NASA'S
ADVANCED SUPERCOMPUTING (NAS)

CHAPTER 7:
PROJECT CONTEXT
NAS AND THE PMO MANDATE

CORE IDEA

NASA's Advanced Supercomputing (NAS) Division transitioned from an operations-centric model to a project-based management environment to meet new demands for complexity, visibility, and agility.

The establishment of the PMO at NAS demonstrates that structured projectization can thrive even in highly technical, mission-critical, government settings—when implemented with a lightweight, business-friendly approach.

1. Background and Mission

- NAS at Ames Research Center delivers one of the world's most advanced high-performance computing environments for scientific and engineering research.
- Supports disciplines from weather modeling to space exploration, requiring massive computational throughput, security, and precision.

- Historically operated as a service-centric organization —effective for stability, but limited in flexibility and cross-disciplinary coordination.

2. Why Projectization Was Necessary

Key Drivers

- Increasing Complexity: Projects like GPU cluster integrations, secure enclave builds, and data-center upgrades required coordination across multiple teams.
- Stakeholder Visibility: Leadership demanded real-time insight into progress, risks, and resourcing.
- Resource Alignment: Evolving priorities and fiscal constraints required adaptable, accountable allocation of assets.
  - The shift to a project economy model became essential for speed, transparency, and resource optimization.

3. The PMO Mandate

The NAS PMO was created with three clear goals:

- Standardization: Adopt one-page charters, risk registers, and communication plans for every project.
- Transparency: Establish dashboards, variance tracking, and weekly dependency stand-ups.
- Governance: Implement lightweight change control for scope and dependency management.

Philosophy: Governance should *enable*, not *constrain*, execution.

4. Business-Friendly Practices

- Simplicity: Templates reduced from dozens of pages to concise, visual summaries.
- Cadence: Weekly stand-ups and portfolio reviews replaced long report-outs.
- Framework Flexibility: Hybrid Agile–Waterfall models supported compliance without sacrificing iteration.
- Culture: Focus on collaboration, clarity, and accountability—not bureaucracy.

Stephen Covey's "Put First Things First" guided prioritization: concentrate on value over volume and allocate resources to the highest-impact work.

5. Leadership Lessons

- Prioritize what matters most; avoid resource dilution.
- Foster trust through transparency and early issue identification.
- Reinforce decision rights and clear ownership.
- Align communication rhythms with execution cadence to sustain momentum.

Covey's focus on prioritization and proactive discipline became the behavioral blueprint for NAS leadership.

6. Results and Early Wins

Within the first year of PMO operation:

- Cycle Times Reduced: Clear charters and defined milestones accelerated delivery.
- Forecast Accuracy Improved: Variance tracking sharpened predictability.
- Stakeholder Satisfaction Rose: Dashboards and weekly status reports increased confidence.
- Cross-Team Collaboration: Shared visibility turned potential bottlenecks into joint problem-solving sessions.

7. Key Takeaways for Other Organizations

- Clarity Beats Complexity: Simple tools and consistent templates outperform elaborate processes.
- Lightweight Governance Works: Accountability without bureaucracy preserves speed.
- Communication Is the Operating System: Embed visibility and dialogue from day one.
- Value Over Volume: Fewer projects with clearer purpose yield stronger results.
- Projectization is Universal: Structured management is as relevant to public science as to private enterprise.

8. Conclusion

The NAS PMO illustrates that project-based management strengthens mission delivery when executed thoughtfully.

By combining clarity, transparency, and lightweight

governance, NAS achieved measurable gains in efficiency and alignment.

This case proves that projectization is not merely a corporate trend but a mission enabler for government and research environments alike.

Result: Innovation and control can co-exist when leadership focuses on clarity and communication.

9. Key Themes

Theme	Summary
Strategic Shift	From service model to project model for flexibility and visibility.
Complexity Management	PMO enabled coordination across technical disciplines.
Transparency & Alignment	Dashboards and weekly updates built confidence.
Lightweight Governance	One-page charters, short stand-ups, hybrid frameworks.
Leadership Discipline	Covey's "Put First Things First" kept focus on value.
Measurable Outcomes	Shorter cycle times, better forecasts, happier stakeholders.
Replicable Model	Simplicity and communication are transferable success factors.

10. Memorable Quotes

- "Put First Things First." —Stephen Covey
- "Plans are only good intentions unless they immediately degenerate into hard work." —Peter Drucker
- "The ability to concentrate and to use your time well is everything." —Lee Iacocca

- "Clarity is kindness." —Modern PMO Principle echoed at NAS

CHAPTER 8: RATIONALE, SCOPE, AND GOVERNANCE

CORE IDEA

The NASA NAS PMO succeeded because it grounded its new model in three clarifying pillars: Rationale (why), Scope (what), and Governance (how).

Together, these turned the PMO from an idea into an operational system that delivered transparency, predictability, and disciplined execution without bureaucracy.

1. Rationale: Why Projectization Was Essential

NAS leaders faced accelerating technical and organizational pressures:

- Rising Complexity: GPU integrations, secure enclaves, and data-center upgrades demanded cross-disciplinary coordination.

- Visibility Requirements: NASA sponsors and federal oversight bodies needed real-time status and risk data.
- Resource Optimization: Budget cycles and limited engineering talent required alignment with the highest-value work.

Purpose of the PMO Formation

To give leaders visibility, teams predictability, and the organization a repeatable framework for delivering complex projects on time and within scope.

A clear "why" anchors every decision and builds stakeholder trust.

2. Scope: Defining What's In and Out

Early discipline around boundaries prevented scope creep and political overreach.

In Scope: Infrastructure upgrades, hardware refreshes, network changes, and major software integrations within NAS.

Out of Scope: Agency-wide policy changes, science deliverables outside NAS, and wholesale tooling overhauls (initially).

This focus enabled quick wins and proof-of-concept.

Lee Iacocca: *"Start with small victories. They build momentum and credibility."*

3. Governance: Structure That Enables Speed

Governance defined how decisions were made without slowing execution.

Core Mechanisms

Governance Element	Purpose	Cadence
Project Charter Approval	One-page charter review by PMO lead + technical sponsor	Per project
Change Control Board (CCB)	Evaluates scope changes & resource shifts → logged for transparency	Biweekly
Dependency Stand-Ups	Surface cross-project risks and sync schedules	Weekly 15 min
Portfolio Reviews	Reprioritize and reallocate resources strategically	Quarterly

Decision Flow Example: A GPU upgrade requiring network changes → PM submits form → CCB evaluates impact → decision logged and communicated within days.

Outcome: Speed with accountability.

4. Leadership and Culture

- Stephen Covey's "Think Win-Win": Governance framed as shared protection, not top-down control.
- Kogon & Blakemore: Keep processes short, clear, and empowering.
- Short meetings + simple templates = engagement and trust.

Governance became a safety net, not a straitjacket.

5. Early Outcomes

- Fewer mid-project delays through proactive dependency reviews.

- Improved sponsor confidence via transparent change logs.
- Higher team satisfaction from fast, documented decisions.
- Predictable delivery for mission-critical initiatives.

6. Lessons for Other Organizations

- Rationale Anchors Change: Define why before how.
- Scope Focuses Effort: Start small, prove value, then expand.
- Governance Drives Speed: Clear decision rights reduce bottlenecks.
- Culture Enables Governance: Frame oversight as empowerment.
- Altucher's Principle: *"Create your own runway."* Build internal discipline before external pressure forces it.

7. Conclusion

Rationale defines purpose. Scope sets focus. Governance creates the decision engine.

Together, they transform a PMO from a concept to a value producer.

NAS proved that clarity and discipline accelerate innovation.

Lee Iacocca: *"The ability to concentrate and to use your time well is everything."*

Governance is that discipline in action—keeping attention on what matters most.

8. Key Themes

Theme	Summary
Rationale	Defined the strategic why for projectization under growing complexity.
Scope	Early boundaries prevented overreach and built momentum through small wins.
Governance	Provided decision rights and accountability without bureaucracy.
Culture & Leadership	Covey's win-win mindset turned oversight into empowerment.
Results	Faster decisions, greater visibility, higher satisfaction.
Transferable Lesson	Lightweight governance and clear scope work in any sector.

9. Memorable Quotes

- *"Think Win-Win."* —Stephen Covey
- *"Start with small victories. They build momentum and credibility."* —Lee Iacocca
- *"Create your own runway."* —James Altucher
- *"The ability to concentrate and to use your time well is everything."* —Lee Iacocca

CHAPTER 9: METHODS, MEASURES, AND FINDINGS

CORE IDEA

A Project Management Office earns credibility not from its structure, but from its evidence of impact.

The NASA NAS PMO established this credibility by pairing quantitative metrics with qualitative insights, proving that effective projectization is as much about culture and communication as it is about data and process.

1. Methods: Measuring What Matters

Mixed-Method Approach:

To capture both performance and perception, the PMO used quantitative data and qualitative feedback in tandem.

Quantitative Methods:

- Cycle Time Analysis: Measured schedule efficiency by comparing planned vs. actual completion dates.
- Forecast Accuracy: Analyzed baseline vs. current variance to identify bias or estimation gaps.
- Resource Utilization: Tracked engineering hours and hardware allocations to balance workload.
- Risk Closure Rate: Monitored mitigation timeliness across projects.

Qualitative Methods:

- Stakeholder Interviews: Collected feedback from scientists, engineers, and sponsors on clarity and decision speed.
- Team Retrospectives: Captured lessons learned and surfaced cultural friction points.
- Observation of Rituals: Evaluated meetings (stand-ups, reviews, CCBs) for transparency and engagement.

Covey's "Put First Things First" guided the focus—measure what truly drives mission success.

2. Core Measures

Rather than drowning in data, the PMO tracked five mission-linked indicators:

- Throughput: Projects completed per quarter.
- Forecast Accuracy: % finishing within ±10% of planned schedule.

- Dependency Risk Index: Weighted score of unresolved inter-project risks.
- Stakeholder Satisfaction: Ratings via Lessons Learned sessions.
- Process Adoption Rate: % of projects using standardized PM tools (charter, risk register, comms plan).

Fewer metrics → sharper focus → better decisions.

3. Findings: Evidence of Progress

- Projects with charters showed 25% higher forecast accuracy.
- Weekly dependency stand-ups reduced mid-project delays.
- One-page status reports increased stakeholder satisfaction.
- Engineers reported clearer priorities and growing trust in leadership decisions.

Insight:

Quantitative improvement and qualitative confidence grew together—metrics worked because they were coupled with meaning.

4. Cultural Resistance and Human Factors

Change wasn't purely technical—it was psychological.

The PMO's top-down rollout initially created resistance.

Challenges:

- Limited Inclusion: Processes were defined *for* engineers, not *with* them.
- Perceived Control: Staff saw documentation as bureaucracy, not support.
- Silent Frustration: Leadership missed early warning signs of disengagement.

Peter Drucker: "The most important thing in communication is hearing what isn't said."

Unheard frustration undermined otherwise strong technical design.

5. Friction at the Front Line

- Teams viewed new tools as administrative overhead.
- Communication felt one-way; leadership talking *at*, not *with*.
- Compliance replaced conviction: tasks were completed, but motivation lagged.
- The early governance model was seen as control, not collaboration.

Result: Work moved forward—but without shared ownership or energy.

6. The Turning Point: From Control to Cooperation

As feedback loops opened and leadership listened, adoption shifted from compliance to commitment.

Engineer feedback: "The templates felt like extra work at first, but now they save time because everyone knows where to find the latest information."

Key Lesson:

Discipline feels like friction before it feels like efficiency.

True transformation began when staff voices shaped process design.

Henry Gantt's Principle:

"Efficiency must be based on cooperation, not coercion."

When cooperation replaced enforcement, engagement and trust returned.

7. Lightweight Governance vs. Heavy-Handed Control

Kory Kogon & Suzette Blakemore: Governance should empower, not constrain.

- Lightweight structure (short meetings, clear templates) saved time.
- Two-way communication converted skepticism into participation.
- Guardrails replaced handcuffs; accountability coexisted with autonomy.

Outcome:

Governance became a shared language—not a compliance exercise.

8. Leadership Insights

Lee Iacocca: "Management is nothing more than motivating other people."

- Data built credibility; leadership built motivation.
- Metrics became conversation tools, not compliance checks.
- Leaders celebrated wins and used patterns to address root issues, not assign blame.

James Altucher's "Idea Machine" Mindset:

Treat each metric as an experiment—test, learn, and scale what works.

Example: dependency stand-ups proved effective → rolled out NAS-wide.

9. Lessons for Other Organizations

- Co-create, don't impose. Engage end users early.
- Close feedback loops. Let staff see how their input changes processes.
- Communicate the "why." Purpose drives participation.
- Start small. Pilot, measure, refine—scale what succeeds.
- Empower over enforce. Authority earns commitment through trust, not pressure.

In the project economy, culture isn't "soft." It's the infrastructure of execution.

10. Conclusion

Measurement validated change, but empathy sustained it.

The NAS PMO proved that data + dialogue = durable transformation.

Covey's "Sharpen the Saw" captures this evolution: continuous improvement through reflection, renewal, and refinement.

Metrics clarified performance; collaboration built culture.

Together, they created a high-trust, high-transparency project environment—one capable of sustaining NASA's mission pace.

11. Key Themes

Theme	Summary
Evidence-Based Credibility	PMO success was proven through balanced metrics, not opinion.
Focused Measurement	Five key indicators are tied directly to mission outcomes.
Data-Driven Insight	Charters, stand-ups, and concise reports measurably improved performance.
Human Resistance	Top-down rollout created compliance, not conviction.
Turning Point	Listening and co-creation shifted adoption from forced to organic.
Governance Balance	Lightweight, human-centered governance enabled speed and trust.
Leadership Role	Leaders are motivated through transparency, not enforcement.
Continuous Learning	Metrics used as hypotheses: measure, adapt, and iterate.

12. Memorable Quotes

- "The most important thing in communication is hearing what isn't said." —Peter Drucker
- "Efficiency must be based on cooperation, not coercion." —Henry Gantt
- "Management is nothing more than motivating other people." —Lee Iacocca
- "Put First Things First." —Stephen Covey

- "Create your own runway." —James Altucher

CHAPTER 10: ETHICS, CONSENT, AND DIGNITY IN ORGANIZATIONAL CHANGE

CORE IDEA

Projectization isn't only structural—it's human.

A PMO succeeds when leaders embed consent, transparency, autonomy, equity, and inclusion into how change is designed, communicated, and governed. Ethics isn't a "nice-to-have"; it's a performance multiplier and a trust engine.

1. The Ethical Imperative

- Change disrupts roles, routines, and identities.
- Ethical leadership safeguards dignity, respects agency, and ensures change is both practical and fair.
- Outcomes must include human outcomes—psychological safety, clarity, and inclusion—not only delivery metrics.

2. Core Ethical Principles

- Informed Consent: Explain what projectization means for roles; invite input before finalizing processes.
- Transparency: Open visibility into decisions, metrics, and resourcing; docs accessible to all.
- Respect for Autonomy: Encourage team-led micro-pivots and local improvements.
- Equity & Inclusion: Rotate opportunities (e.g., leading initiatives, presenting at portfolio reviews) to prevent favoritism.

3. Practical Applications

- Open Forums/Q&A with leadership to surface concerns.
- Feedback Loops: anonymous surveys + structured dialogues; close the loop with visible adjustments.
- Consent in Data Use: clear policies on how performance data is collected, stored, and shared.

Covey: "Seek First to Understand, Then to Be Understood." Listening precedes design.

4. Balancing Speed with Humanity

- Rapid launches can exclude or pressure teams.
- Add a Stakeholder Impact & Acknowledgment section to each charter (affected leads sign/acknowledge).

- Create room for urgency and dignity; fast doesn't mean opaque.

5. Qualitative Insights (Trust Dynamics)

- People don't need to agree with every decision—but they must understand how it was made.
- Trust grows through consistent explanation, transparent trade-offs, and visible response to feedback.
- Transparency transforms resistance into dialogue; credibility shifts decisions from "theirs" to "ours."

Drucker: "The truly dangerous thing is asking the wrong questions." Attend to unspoken concerns.

6. Lessons for Leaders

- Own the downside (Altucher): anticipate human costs and mitigate them upfront.
- Unofficial PMs (Kogon & Blakemore) depend on relationships, not hierarchy → ethics is non-negotiable.
- Make ethics operational: who is impacted, how consent is sought, and where feedback changes design.

7. Governance as an Ethical Tool

- Charters, CCBs, risk registers = safeguards for dignity, not bureaucratic hurdles.

- Clear documentation reduces rumors; scheduled feedback reduces anxiety; transparent decisions build trust.
- Ethical governance = cooperation over coercion; clarity over compliance theater.

8. Conclusion

Ethics is a strategic advantage in a projectized world.

When PMOs embed consent, transparency, autonomy, and inclusion, organizations move faster with integrity.

Ethics and efficiency aren't opposing forces—they reinforce each other and sustain long-term performance.

9. Key Themes

Theme	Summary
Human-Centered Change	Projectization impacts identities—treat people as partners, not passengers.
Consent & Transparency	Explain changes, invite input, and show how feedback shaped outcomes.
Autonomy & Inclusion	Empower micro-pivots; distribute opportunities fairly.
Speed with Safety	Build stakeholder acknowledgment into charters; move fast without sidelining people.
Trust as Accelerator	Understanding the "why" increases commitment and execution speed.
Governance as Safeguard	Use PM tools to protect dignity and reduce rumors, not to control.

10. Memorable Quotes

- "Seek first to understand, then to be understood." — Stephen Covey
- "The truly dangerous thing is asking the wrong questions." —Peter Drucker
- "Own the downside." —James Altucher
- "The ability to work effectively with people is as critical as technical competence." —PMO principle echoed in this chapter

NOTES
LEADING THE WORK

CHAPTER 11: PROJECT LEADERSHIP: FROM FORMING TO PERFORMING

CORE IDEA

Frameworks, tools, and charters provide structure—but leadership transforms structure into success.

In every project, leadership is the catalyst that turns plans into performance, especially as teams move through the natural phases of forming, storming, norming, and performing.

1. Leadership as the Bridge Between Planning and Execution

- Projects fail not because of flawed methodology but because of gaps in leadership behavior.
- Great leaders translate vision into clarity, uncertainty into confidence, and conflict into collaboration.
- Leadership bridges the gap between *technical process* and *human performance*.

Jack Welch: "Good business leaders create a vision, articulate the vision, passionately own the vision, and relentlessly drive it to completion."

2. Understanding Team Dynamics (Tuckman's Model)

Bruce Tuckman's framework remains one of the most practical guides for project leaders managing evolving teams:

Phase	Leadership Focus	Outcome
Forming	Clarify purpose, roles, and expectations; create psychological safety.	Alignment and engagement.
Storming	Normalize conflict; mediate issues early; maintain focus on mission.	Healthy dialogue replaces tension.
Norming	Reinforce trust; solidify working agreements; delegate more.	Stability and shared ownership.
Performing	Empower autonomy; coach rather than direct; remove barriers.	High performance and innovation.

Recognizing storming as a sign of growth, not dysfunction, prevents leaders from overcorrecting or losing trust during conflict.

3. People Before Process

Stephen Covey's 7 Habits provide timeless human-centered leadership principles:

- *Be Proactive*: anticipate and act before issues escalate.

- *Begin with the End in Mind*: keep vision and success metrics visible.
- *Seek First to Understand*: practice empathetic listening.
- *Synergize*: leverage diversity for stronger outcomes.
- *Sharpen the Saw*: sustain personal growth and energy.

Leadership grounded in empathy and trust creates enduring performance.

4. Practical Leadership Tactics

Vision Casting: Start every project with a clear "why" that connects the mission to meaning.

Meeting Facilitation: Open with desired outcomes; time-box discussions; close with decisions.

Conflict Resolution: Treat conflict as valuable data; seek win-win outcomes.

Motivation: Offer frequent recognition and visibility; build confidence through acknowledgment.

Decision Clarity: Document key decisions and ownership within 24 hours to prevent drift.

These repeatable, behavioral habits create *daily momentum* and a culture of accountability.

5. Leading Without Title

- Kory Kogon and Suzette Blakemore stress that leadership is a *behavior, not a position*.

- "Unofficial project leaders" succeed through influence, trust, and credibility rather than hierarchy.
- They act as connectors—aligning teams, resolving friction, and enabling outcomes across functions.

In projectized environments, *influence leadership* is often more powerful than positional authority.

6. Technology as a Leadership Amplifier

- Collaboration tools (Teams, Asana, Jira, etc.) accelerate visibility but require clear digital etiquette.
- Define which tools are used for decisions, discussion, and status updates.
- Set expectations for responsiveness and communication tone.

Technology amplifies leadership clarity—but also exposes weak leadership if boundaries are unclear.

7. Case Example: Dependency Stand-Ups

At NASA's NAS PMO, weekly dependency stand-ups became a leadership model:

- 15-minute cadence focused on blockers, not updates.
- Action orientation: who owns what, by when.
- Transparency: shared visibility into dependencies and progress.

This "cadence of clarity" built cross-team trust, accelerated issue resolution, and established a rhythm of accountability.

8. Empowerment Drives Innovation

- James Altucher's "idea machine" principle: empower teams to solve, not wait for direction.
- Empowerment converts compliance into creativity and ownership.
- Leaders build systems where people feel safe experimenting and learning fast.

"When people understand the why, they'll figure out the how." —Project Leader Reflection

9. Leadership as Communication in Action

- Consistent, transparent communication is the most effective leadership behavior.
- Communication establishes alignment, builds trust, and sustains morale.
- The best leaders don't just share updates—they *share understanding.*

Communication is not an accessory to leadership; it is leadership in action.

10. From Forming to Performing: The Leadership Journey

- Teams evolve through predictable stages; effective leaders guide them intentionally.
- Forming to Performing is not automatic—it requires clarity, empathy, and disciplined rhythm.

- The true measure of leadership is not control but creating conditions for others to thrive.

The leader's role: build trust, set clear direction, and remove obstacles so the team can perform.

11. Key Themes

Theme	Summary
Leadership Bridges Method and Mindset	Methodology provides tools; leadership activates people.
Tuckman's Framework	Recognize and lead through Forming–Storming–Norming–Performing.
Covey's Habits in Action	Empathy, proactivity, and renewal sustain long-term success.
Practical Behaviors	Vision, facilitation, recognition, and clarity drive day-to-day performance.
Leadership Without Title	Influence and credibility outperform positional authority.
Technology with Discipline	Tools amplify good leadership when used with clear norms.
Cadence of Clarity	Predictable communication builds trust and speed.
Empowerment = Innovation	Encourage teams to ideate and own their results.

12. Memorable Quotes

- "When people understand the why, they'll figure out the how." —NASA PM Reflection
- "The ability to concentrate and to use your time well is everything." —Lee Iacocca

- "Good business leaders create a vision, articulate the vision, passionately own the vision, and relentlessly drive it to completion." —Jack Welch
- "Synergize." —Stephen Covey
- "Leadership is not a title; it's a behavior." —Kory Kogon & Suzette Blakemore

CHAPTER 12: CULTURE, DOCUMENTATION, AND MENTORING

CORE IDEA

Project frameworks may define how work is organized, but culture determines how people behave within them.

Sustainable success comes from integrating three forces: culture (which builds trust), documentation (which preserves wisdom), and mentoring (which multiplies knowledge).

Together, they create the backbone of a resilient, projectized organization.

1. The Power of Culture

- Culture is the sum of daily behaviors, not slogans or policies.
- *Stephen Covey:* culture = "collective habits."
- When those habits promote transparency, respect, and accountability, projects thrive.

- Strong cultures foster psychological safety—where people can raise issues, admit mistakes, and question assumptions without fear.
- *Bill Campbell* coached leaders to make conflict constructive and candor safe.
- *Lee Iacocca:* "The ability to get along with people is as important as being technically competent."

Practical Cultural Practices

- Open Reviews: turn portfolio meetings into learning conversations.
- Voice Equity: ensure junior and senior voices are equally heard.
- Celebrate Micro-Wins: reinforce progress, build momentum, and humanize leadership.

Leadership shows up in daily interactions—how you listen, recognize, and respond.

2. Documentation as Knowledge Infrastructure

Culture creates openness; documentation creates continuity.

"What isn't documented can't be transferred" —Kogon & Blakemore.

Core Artifacts

Artifact	Purpose
Project Charter	Defines purpose, scope, and milestones.
Risk Register	Tracks issues and mitigations.
Decision Log	Records critical decisions and rationale.
Lessons Learned Canvas	Captures insights for future projects.

Best Practices

- Keep documentation lightweight but structured.
- Store artifacts in shared, searchable repositories.
- Tie documentation milestones to project phases.
- Treat documentation as a leadership behavior, not clerical work.

Peter Drucker: "What gets measured gets managed."

Likewise, *what gets documented gets preserved.*

3. The Risks of Tribal Knowledge

Relying on informal know-how ("tribal knowledge") introduces fragility.

Risk	Impact
Single Points of Failure	Projects stall when key people leave.
Reinventing the Wheel	Rework and lost learning.
Inconsistent Execution	Quality drifts; standards diverge.
Slow Onboarding	New hires learn by rumor, delaying progress.
Poor Decision Recall	Forgotten rationale leads to confusion.
Hero Dependence	A few "indispensables" hold knowledge hostage.

Shift:

From *tribal memory* → *institutional memory*.

From *heroes* → *systems.*

4. Turning Knowledge into Infrastructure

- Embed documentation checkpoints into lifecycle (charter → risk log → close-out report).
- Apply light but mandatory standards for consistency.
- Use centralized, searchable repositories linked to collaboration tools.
- Reward documentation efforts in evaluations and recognition programs.

Bill Campbell: Clear communication isn't bureaucracy; it's empowerment.

Documentation removes friction and accelerates better decisions.

5. Mentoring as Cultural Glue

Knowledge lives through people as much as through systems.

Mentoring accelerates learning and reinforces cultural norms.

Effective Mentoring Guidelines

- Encourage reverse mentoring—junior staff share fresh tech or perspectives.
- Pair mentors and mentees across disciplines to dissolve silos.
- Recognize and reward mentors in reviews to institutionalize learning.

Bill Campbell's legacy: Leaders are coaches first.

Mentorship scales leadership and keeps culture alive.

- *James Altucher:* Mentorship creates a "network effect"—each connection amplifies collective capability.

6. Integration of Culture and Documentation

- Culture and documentation reinforce each other:
  - Openness → honest records.

  - Clear records → trust & safety.
- Covey's "Sharpen the Saw"—continually renew systems of knowledge and mentorship.
- Knowledge renewal keeps organizations agile in fast-moving project economies.

7. Lessons for Leaders

- Model the Behavior: contribute directly to risk registers and decision logs.
- Coach Openly: make documentation and feedback visible.
- Mentor Intentionally: invest time developing others; don't delegate it away.
- *Bill Campbell:* "You can't coach what you don't live."
- Leadership presence > policy presence.

When leaders embody culture, document their decisions, and mentor consistently, they build organizational muscle memory—habits that persist beyond any single project.

8. Conclusion

- Culture enables trust.
- Documentation preserves wisdom.
- Mentorship sustains both.

These three elements transform transient projects into enduring capability.

Strong leaders—like Bill Campbell, Peter Drucker, and Jack Welch—teach that authentic leadership is care in action.

The project leader's mission extends beyond delivery: to leave behind a culture where knowledge flows freely, people grow, and success replicates itself.

9. Key Themes

Theme	Summary
Culture Drives Outcomes	Openness and respect turn frameworks into value.
Psychological Safety	Candor and vulnerability enable innovation.
Documentation = Continuity	Preserves decisions and accelerates onboarding.
Tribal Knowledge = Fragility	Without documentation, progress is temporary.
Mentorship Multiplies Impact	Personal coaching transfers tacit knowledge and builds trust.
Leaders Model the Way	Participation and visibility make cultural values real.
Integration Yields Resilience	Culture + Documentation + Mentoring = long-term strength.

10. Memorable Quotes

- "Culture is the collective habits of an organization." —Stephen Covey
- "The ability to get along with people is as important as being technically competent." —Lee Iacocca
- "What gets measured gets managed." —Peter Drucker
- "You can't coach what you don't live." —Bill Campbell

- "Good business leaders create a vision, articulate the vision, passionately own the vision, and relentlessly drive it to completion." —Jack Welch

CHAPTER 13: SCHEDULING WITHOUT TIME TRAVEL

CORE IDEA

A schedule isn't a prediction of perfection—it's a living contract of expectations.

When timelines drift from reality, project leaders must choose: preserve the illusion or tell the truth.

Scheduling without time travel means aligning the plan to reality, not bending reality to fit the plan.

1. The Real Purpose of a Schedule

A schedule is not a wish list or a work of fiction—it's a commitment framework between the team and its stakeholders.

A good schedule does three things:

- Clarifies work, sequencing, and interdependencies.
- Surfaces risks before they become crises.

- Guides decisions in real time.

Stephen Covey: "Begin with the End in Mind."

A schedule's purpose is not to protect optimism—it's to guide execution toward the agreed outcome.

A false schedule is dangerous. It:

- Creates complacency.
- Misleads leadership.
- Erases accountability.

2. Technical Foundations

Technique	Purpose
Work Breakdown Structure (WBS)	Defines the scope and logical structure of work.
Critical Path Method (CPM)	Identifies which tasks truly drive project duration.
Float/Slack Analysis	Shows where delay can occur without impact.
Buffers & Contingencies	Absorb surprises from the "real world."

Anchor your plan in reality rather than wishful thinking.

3. Practical Habits for Realistic Forecasting

- Effort-Driven Estimates: Base durations on available people and actual hours.
- Progressive Elaboration: Refine as you learn—let the schedule evolve.

- Short Task Durations: Smaller chunks = faster measurement and accountability.
- Regular Updates: Stale schedules breed time paradoxes.
- Transparent Variances: Report slips early; reality heals faster than silence.

James Altucher: "Iterate in small bets."

Frequent, honest adjustments beat long stretches of fantasy planning.

4. When Time Travel Happens

You'll know you've entered the scheduling multiverse when:

- Tasks start before their start date.
- Tasks end before they're finished.
- "Complete" work still shows as "future."

These paradoxes destroy trust and accuracy.

The fix:

1. Acknowledge the variance.
2. Explain the cause.
3. Propose corrective actions.
4. Adjust the schedule to reflect the truth.

A schedule that matches reality earns trust.

A schedule that hides reality loses credibility.

5. Tools and Technology

Tools enable clarity—but don't enforce honesty.

Examples:

- Microsoft Project, Primavera, Smartsheet: Predictive modeling, dependency visualization.
- Kanban Boards / Agile Dashboards: Real-time task status and flow visibility.

Rule:

When predictive schedules and live boards match, you have truth.

When they diverge, you have a paradox to fix.

6. Human Factors

The real challenge isn't in the Gantt chart—it's in the culture.

Teams need psychological safety to admit when timelines drift.

Without it, people will quietly "fix the data" to match expectations rather than reality.

Trust > Fiction. Always.

Leaders must model honesty: acknowledging slippage early signals maturity, not weakness.

7. Fun with Time Travel: The Paradox Example

Classic scenario:

- Task X, scheduled for next Friday, starts *yesterday.*
- Task Y is marked "complete," but the finish date is *next Tuesday.*

Your schedule just became a DeLorean dashboard.

When leaders tolerate these paradoxes, they manage ghost work—tasks that exist only in reports.

Fix the flux capacitor:

- Update start and finish dates.
- Recalculate dependencies.
- Let the timeline tell the true story.

8. Leadership Application

Scheduling is leadership in action.

The maturity of a PMO can be measured by how well its schedules reflect the truth.

Leadership behaviors that reinforce schedule realism:

- Communicate slippages calmly and early.
- Align updates with facts, not optimism.
- Reinforce that transparency > punishment.
- Keep leadership informed, not surprised.

Lee Iacocca: "The ability to concentrate and to use your time well is everything."

A realistic schedule channels that concentration into results.

9. Key Themes

Theme	Summary
Schedules Are Contracts, Not Fantasies	They define expectations and guide delivery—not dreams.
Realism Over Optimism	Trust grows when timelines reflect reality, even if imperfect.
Classic PM Techniques Still Work	WBS, CPM, Float, and Buffers remain foundational.
Short, Frequent, Transparent Updates	Replace long-range fiction with near-term truth.
Psychological Safety Enables Accuracy	Teams must feel safe to report real progress and slippage.
Technology = Amplifier, Not Solution	Tools reflect data; culture determines honesty.
Leadership = Schedule Integrity	Mature leaders fix the paradox, not the optics.

10. Memorable Quotes

- "Begin with the End in Mind." —Stephen Covey
- "Iterate in small bets." —James Altucher
- "The ability to concentrate and to use your time well is everything." —Lee Iacocca
- "Trust > Fiction. Always." —Project Paradigm Principle

CHAPTER 14: DEPENDENCIES AND RISK: "BEFORE THE FIRST DOMINO FALLS"

CORE IDEA

Projects rarely collapse from a single catastrophic event—they fail by accumulation.

A missing approval, a delayed shipment, or an overbooked engineer each seems small until one triggers another, creating a domino effect.

Dependency and risk management are not back-office exercises—they are leadership disciplines that turn complexity into visibility and prevent collapse before it begins.

1. Understanding Dependencies

A dependency exists anytime the start or finish of one task relies on another.

Recognizing these connections early allows leaders to anticipate constraints and protect the critical path.

Type	Description	Example
Technical	One component must be completed before another begins.	Software must pass testing before deployment.
Resource	Shared personnel or tools constrain sequencing.	A key engineer supports two projects.
Decision	Approvals or sign-offs gate progress.	Procurement waits for leadership approval.
External	Outside vendors, customers, or regulators influence timing.	Supplier delivery or agency review.

Leadership takeaway: Dependencies are *early warnings* of future risk—the first cracks before the dam breaks.

2. Tools for Managing Dependencies

- Dependency Register: Living record of dependencies, owners, and due dates.
- Network Diagrams: Visualize task linkages and critical path sensitivity.
- Interface Control Documents (ICDs): Define cross-team or system responsibilities.

Practical Dependency Tactics

- Weekly Dependency Stand-Ups: 15-minute cross-team syncs to flag blockers.

- Color-Coded Dashboards: Red–Yellow–Green indicators for at-risk dependencies.
- Early Warning Signals: Reward early reporting; "early is good, late is expensive."

Dependencies are leading indicators—manage them, and you manage risk before it manifests.

3. Risk Management: The PMI Framework

According to the PMBOK® Guide, risk management is a systematic, repeatable process for handling uncertainty.

PMI's 7 Processes:

- Plan Risk Management: Define methods, roles, and reporting cadence.
- Identify Risks: Use brainstorming, expert input, and assumption analysis.
- Perform Qualitative Analysis: Prioritize by probability and impact.
- Perform Quantitative Analysis: Use Monte Carlo or EMV to gauge exposure.
- Plan Risk Responses:
  - *Avoid*: remove the threat.
  - *Mitigate*: reduce likelihood/impact.
  - *Transfer*: shift ownership (e.g., vendor, insurance).
  - *Accept*: monitor and tolerate.
  - *Exploit/Enhance/Share*: for positive risks (opportunities).
- Implement Responses: Execute mitigation actions.

- Monitor Risks: Track triggers, update registers, and communicate status.

Key Tools

- Risk Register: Repository of risks, owners, impacts, and mitigations.
- Probability-Impact Matrix: Visual prioritization grid.
- Risk Breakdown Structure (RBS): Hierarchical categorization.
- Risk Burn-Down Chart: Progress tracker for mitigation over time.

Stephen Covey's Habit 1—"Be Proactive"—defines good risk leadership: anticipate the iceberg before it hits the ship.

4. Integrating Dependencies and Risks

In practice, dependencies and risks are two sides of the same coin.

Relationship	Example
Delayed Dependency = Realized Risk	Vendor delay triggers schedule slip.
Fragile Dependency = Potential Risk	Only one supplier for key hardware.
Critical Dependency = Risk Amplifier	One bottleneck affects multiple milestones.

Integration Practices

- Linked Registers: Cross-reference dependencies within the risk register.
- Joint Dashboards: Show both dependency health and risk probability in one view.
- Impact Forecasting: Auto-update risk scores when dependencies shift.
- Scenario Planning: "What-if" sessions to test mitigation readiness.

Example:

If GPU hardware delivery depends on a single vendor:

- *Dependency Register:* "Vendor A shipment of GPU boards."
- *Risk Register:* "Vendor delay $\rightarrow$ 3-week slip in cluster build."
  - Mitigation: Pre-qualify Vendor B or reorder task sequence.

When registers "talk," leaders see the *system*, not just the symptoms.

5. Communication and Culture

Tools reveal data—culture reveals truth.

Dependencies and risks thrive in silence, not spreadsheets.

Effective Review Cadence

Focus each review on:

- What changed since last week?

- What new risks have emerged?
- What mitigations are working or failing?
- What decisions are required?

Lee Iacocca: "Management is nothing more than motivating other people."

Create a no-blame culture in which surfacing risk is rewarded rather than punished.

6. Leadership Lessons

- Identify cross-team dependencies during chartering, not midstream.
- Assign clear ownership—every risk and dependency has one accountable leader.
- Combine qualitative and quantitative methods for decision confidence.
- Foster psychological safety—issues raised early prevent escalation later.
- Integrate dependencies and risks into one view for executive clarity.

Ambiguity is the enemy of mitigation. Clarity is the leader's first duty.

7. Key Themes

Theme	Summary
Dependencies Drive Risk	Every connection between tasks is a potential chain reaction.
Structured Risk Management Works	PMI's 7-step model disciplines uncertainty into action.
Integration = Insight	Linked dashboards and registers create a holistic risk picture.
Ownership Enables Action	Each risk/dependency must have a named owner.
Communication Beats Compliance	Frequent, honest loops prevent silent buildup.
Culture Determines Resilience	A no-blame environment encourages transparency and speed.
Proactive Leadership Prevents Cascades	One early intervention can stop months of recovery effort.

8. Memorable Quotes

- "Be Proactive." —Stephen Covey
- "Management is nothing more than motivating other people." —Lee Iacocca
- "Early is good; late is expensive." —PMO Principle
- "Build your own runway." —James Altucher

9. Summary Insight

Dependencies and risks are not paperwork—they are early-warning systems for leadership.

When leaders connect them, communicate them, and act on them early, they prevent cascades, preserve trust, and keep the first domino from falling.

CHAPTER 15: AI, AUTOMATION, AND THE FUTURE OF PROJECT MANAGEMENT

CORE IDEA

Artificial Intelligence has moved from a future concept to a present capability, reshaping how projects are planned, executed, and monitored.

Yet the rise of intelligent automation does not diminish the human role; it elevates it.

The next generation of project managers will thrive by pairing machine precision with human judgment, ethics, and empathy.

1. AI Across the Project Lifecycle

AI tools now enhance nearly every phase of project delivery—from forecasting to execution control.

Function	AI Contribution
Predictive Scheduling	Algorithms forecast slippage using task data, dependencies, and historical trends.
Automated Reporting	Natural Language Processing (NLP) automatically generates meeting notes, summaries, and dashboards.
Resource Optimization	Machine learning models rebalance staff assignments based on workload, skill, and availability.
Risk Detection	AI scans documents, messages, and logs to surface emerging threats.
Decision Support Dashboards	Synthesizes live data streams into actionable insights for leadership.

Result: AI transforms the project manager's role from data collector to decision strategist.

2. Practical Example: Predict Before You React

Organizations now use AI-driven forecasting to anticipate supply-chain issues or delivery delays.

Instead of reacting to missed deadlines, PMOs can adjust schedules, communicate impacts, and reallocate resources early.

Outcome:

Early visibility → proactive response → reduced cost and disruption.

AI doesn't replace the project manager—it augments their situational awareness.

3. The Human Advantage

Technology delivers data, but humans provide meaning.

AI's analytical power must be balanced by leadership qualities that machines cannot emulate.

Irreplaceable Human Strengths

- Ethical Judgment: Knowing when to trust the algorithm—and when not to.
- Stakeholder Engagement: Building trust around data-driven decisions.
- Creative Problem-Solving: Navigating politics, culture, and ambiguity.
- Motivation & Coaching: Inspiring teams to embrace change confidently.

Stephen Covey's habits—"Seek First to Understand," "Think Win-Win," and "Sharpen the Saw"—are more vital than ever.

4. Balanced Practices: The "Human-in-the-Loop"

AI should inform decisions, not make them.

Example Loop

1. AI analyzes performance and highlights risks.
2. Teams discuss insights and validate context.

3. Leaders make the final decision.
4. Adjustments feed back into the system.

This hybrid model ensures transparency, accountability, and context-awareness.

It prevents automation from drifting into blind trust.

Balance defines maturity: Let data guide, but let humans decide.

5. Opportunities and New Risks

Advantages

- Faster decision cycles
- Sharper risk foresight
- Increased forecasting accuracy
- Reduced reporting burden

Emerging Risks

Category	Description
Data Privacy	Sensitive project data must be protected across automated systems.
Algorithmic Bias	AI reflects the quality and fairness of its training data.
Transparency	Teams must understand *why* an algorithm produces a given output.

Jack Welch: "Control your own destiny or someone else will."

AI-savvy leaders take ownership of their tools and question their logic.

6. Preparing for the Future

To stay relevant, project managers must become AI-literate translators—bridging technology and people.

James Altucher's "Idea Machine" mindset applies directly:

- Learn emerging AI tools and trends.
- Experiment with automation safely and iteratively.
- Strengthen human skills—empathy, negotiation, storytelling, and foresight.
- Understand AI outputs well enough to challenge them intelligently.

Tomorrow's project manager: not a coder, but a *communicator of insight* between humans and machines.

7. Leadership Imperative

Future-ready leaders must:

- Combine data literacy with ethical sensitivity.
- Establish governance frameworks for AI use (data security, transparency, oversight).
- Encourage teams to co-create automation workflows, not just adopt them.
- Keep human values at the core of technical transformation.

Leadership in the AI era = wisdom + awareness + curiosity.

8. Key Themes

Theme	Summary
AI <u>Enhances,</u> Not Replaces	It amplifies leadership capability by automating repetitive work.
Predictive Intelligence = Foresight	AI identifies risks and opportunities before they surface.
Human Judgment Remains Essential	Ethics, empathy, and creativity anchor decision quality.
Human-in-the-Loop Models	Preserve accountability while leveraging automation.
AI Introduces New Risks	Privacy, bias, and transparency require active management.
AI Literacy Is Leadership Literacy	Future PMs must interpret and challenge algorithmic insight.
Humans + Machines = Synergy	The true advantage is collaboration, not competition.

9. Memorable Quotes

- "Seek First to Understand, Then to Be Understood." —Stephen Covey
- "Control your own destiny or someone else will." —Jack Welch
- "Become an idea machine." —James Altucher
- Project Paradigm Principle: "Data guides. Humans decide."

10. Summary Insight

The future of project management isn't *human versus machine*—it's human plus machine.

AI will process, predict, and report. Humans will interpret, motivate, and decide.

Those who embrace the partnership—blending analytical precision with emotional intelligence—will define the next era of project leadership.

NOTES
THE PLAYBOOK

CHAPTER 16: STANDING UP A PMO AND CHANGE BOARD

CORE IDEA

Standing up a Project Management Office (PMO) is as much about culture as it is about structure.

A PMO succeeds when it creates clarity without bureaucracy, provides visibility without micromanagement, and reinforces collaboration through trust.

The addition of a Change Control Board (CCB) strengthens governance by making decision-making transparent, consistent, and accountable.

1. Purpose and Vision

A PMO exists to enhance organizational delivery capability—making projects predictable, aligned, and transparent.

Clarity of purpose drives adoption:

- Define *why* the PMO matters (improved predictability, collaboration, and strategy alignment).
- Back up words with actions that prove the PMO simplifies, not complicates, work.
- Link PMO goals directly to organizational value and mission outcomes.

"Vision without execution is hallucination."

A PMO must translate its vision into visible improvements from day one.

2. Implementation Steps

A disciplined, staged approach prevents overload and builds credibility.

Step	Description
1. Charter the PMO	Define mission, services, and metrics. Keep concise and outcome-focused.
2. Start Small	Launch with pilot projects to generate early success stories.
3. Standardize Core Templates	Introduce shared tools (charters, risk logs, status reports).
4. Establish Governance	Create a CCB to review changes and manage dependencies.
5. Set Cadence	Weekly stand-ups, monthly portfolio reviews, quarterly retrospectives.
6. Measure and Adjust	Use data to refine throughput, accuracy, and stakeholder satisfaction.

Stephen Covey's principle "Begin with the End in Mind" applies here: define the PMO's mission as a measurable improvement, not a document.

3. Leadership and Cultural Considerations

The PMO's cultural tone will determine its long-term success.

Leaders must embody Covey's habits to balance structure and collaboration.

Covey-Inspired Leadership Framework

- Seek First to Understand: Listen to stakeholders before defining processes.
- Think Win-Win: Present the PMO as a support partner, not a gatekeeper.
- Synergize: Co-create templates and workflows with functional leads.
- Sharpen the Saw: Invest in continuous training to sustain PM maturity.

Culture determines adoption. Bureaucracy kills momentum.

4. Case Example: NAS Change Board

NASA's NAS Division implemented a lightweight Change Control Board (CCB):

- Cadence: Biweekly, capped at 30 minutes.
- Membership: PMO leads, technical experts, and key stakeholders.
- Transparency: All decisions logged in a shared register.
- Outcome: Faster approvals, clear accountability, and improved coordination.

This structure embodied *"disciplined agility"*—formal enough to ensure traceability, flexible enough to keep work moving.

5. Practical Tips for a Successful Launch

- Communicate Early & Often: Proactive messaging builds trust and reduces resistance.
- Celebrate Early Wins: Publicize successful pilot outcomes to validate the PMO's value.
- Keep Tools Simple: Start with accessible systems (Excel, SharePoint) before complex platforms.
- Empower Unofficial PMs: Coach team leads managing projects informally to extend PMO reach.
- Show Quick ROI: Demonstrate improvements in schedule accuracy and decision velocity.

Momentum builds credibility. Simplicity builds adoption.

6. Lessons Learned

- Deliver Value Quickly: Credibility grows when early results are visible.
- Pilot Before Policy: Start small; refine based on real-world lessons.
- Use Governance for Speed, Not Control: The CCB's purpose is clarity, not bureaucracy.
- Measure What Matters: Forecast accuracy, throughput, satisfaction, and issue resolution rate.
- Model Leadership Behaviors: PMO leaders must show partnership, empathy, and transparency.
- Build Trust Through Communication: Frequent updates reduce uncertainty and encourage collaboration.

Steve Jobs: "Innovation distinguishes between a leader and a follower."

An innovative PMO leads change; it isn't forced to react to it.

7. Key Themes

Theme	Summary
PMO = Structure + Leadership	A PMO standardizes practices while enabling collaboration and trust.
Purpose and Vision Drive Buy-In	People adopt what they understand and believe in.
Start Small, Scale Smart	Pilot success is better than large-scale failure.
Templates Create a Common Language	Shared tools make coordination easier across functions.
Change Control Board Enables Agility	Governance should accelerate—not delay—progress.
Cadence Builds Rhythm	Regular reviews foster alignment and accountability.
Leadership Shapes Culture	Covey's habits transform process into partnership.
Early Wins Create Momentum	Tangible results accelerate executive support.
Simplicity Over Complexity	Start lean; expand only as needs mature.
Empower Informal Leaders	Unofficial PMs multiply PMO influence and adoption.
Innovation and Adaptability	PMOs that evolve stay relevant and resilient.

8. Memorable Quotes

- "Seek First to Understand, Then to Be Understood." —Stephen Covey
- "Innovation distinguishes between a leader and a follower." —Steve Jobs
- "Vision without execution is hallucination." — Thomas Edison (attributed)
- Project Paradigm Principle: "Governance should create momentum, not friction."

9. Summary Insight

Launching a PMO and Change Board is not about bureaucracy—it's about building trust through structure.

When implemented with clarity, purpose, and leadership, the PMO becomes a strategic enabler, improving predictability, empowering collaboration, and aligning execution to mission goals.

Culture, cadence, and credibility are the true engines that sustain it.

CHAPTER 17: PURPOSE-VIEW ALIGNMENT & TASK-TECHNOLOGY FIT

CORE IDEA

Technology is not inherently transformative; alignment is.

In the project economy, the true test of any platform is whether it amplifies clarity, collaboration, and accountability around the project's mission.

The best tool is not the most powerful—it's the one that fits the work, the users, and the purpose.

1. From Technology to Leadership Decision

Technology selection is not an IT decision—it's a strategic leadership act.

When tools are aligned to purpose, they accelerate performance; when misaligned, they create friction.

Bill Walsh built a dynasty by perfecting the "standards of performance."

He focused on precision in systems, not the scoreboard—because "the score takes care of itself."

Likewise, a PMO that aligns purpose and technology achieves predictable success without micromanagement.

2. Linking Purpose to View

Every project tool should begin with one question:

"What decisions must this view enable?"

Purpose-View Connection Framework

Step	Leadership Focus	Example
Define Mission	Clarify what outcomes the tool supports.	Improve cross-team visibility on schedule risk.
Identify Stakeholders	Determine who needs what view.	Executives → Portfolio dashboards; Engineers → Task boards.
Establish Decision Cadence	Align update frequency with decision timing.	Daily stand-ups, weekly risk reviews, quarterly portfolio syncs.

Bill Walsh's Field Vision Analogy:

Just as a quarterback's field view reveals what matters in the moment, well-designed dashboards give leaders decision-ready visibility.

Leadership Principle:

Jocko Willink: "Discipline equals freedom."

Disciplined tool design unlocks flexibility and autonomy in execution.

3. Strategic Alignment Checklist

To ensure technology serves the purpose and people:

- Mission Clarity: What problem or outcome does the tool support?
- Stakeholder Needs: Who needs visibility, and at what level of detail?
- Decision Cadence: How often does information need to drive action?

Eric Schmidt (Trillion Dollar Coach): The goal is to "have the right conversations with the right people at the right time."

Tools should enable those conversations—not just report on them.

4. Task-Technology Fit

Once the purpose and view are clear, the next step is to ensure that the technology fits the tasks it is intended to support.

NASA NAS Example:

The PMO evaluated Jira, Smartsheet, and SharePoint not for popularity but for task suitability—risk tracking, schedule forecasting, and dependency mapping.

The guiding question:

"Which tool best supports the tasks required to deliver mission outcomes?"

Evaluation Rubric

Criterion	Key Question
Ease of Use	Can everyone access and understand the data?
Integration	Does it connect to existing systems and workflows?
Scalability	Will it handle growth across projects and users?
Security & Compliance	Does it meet federal or organizational standards?
Cost vs. Value	Are benefits proportional to expense?

5. Practical Selection Process

A PMO can use a four-step method to ensure disciplined adoption:

1. Define Critical Tasks: Identify core functions (e.g., change control, risk tracking, resource allocation).
2. Pilot the Options: Test tools with real projects to validate fit.
3. Gather Feedback: Include end users in evaluation— adoption starts with inclusion.
4. Train and Iterate: Provide targeted instruction and adjust based on experience.

Extreme Ownership Mindset:

"Leaders must own everything in their world. There is no one else to blame." —Jocko Willink

Tool failure is not a technical issue—it's a leadership accountability gap.

6. Beyond Popularity: Strategic Fit Over Trend

Avoid the "copy-paste" trap: what worked in another company may not work in yours.

Tool performance depends on contextual fit—culture, workflow, and decision rhythm.

Analogy:

A star quarterback may struggle in the wrong offensive system—likewise, a great tool misaligned with your operational tempo will underperform.

Strategic alignment always beats trend adoption.

7. Human Factors: The Decisive Variable

Technology amplifies human behavior; it does not replace it.

Leadership Insights:

- *James Altucher* warns against chasing "shiny objects."
- *Kory Kogon and Suzette Blakemore* emphasize that adoption depends on training and clarity.
- *Bill Campbell* taught: "It's the people." Technology succeeds when people are coached and empowered.
- *Jocko Willink* reinforces: "A disciplined team with average tools will outperform an undisciplined team with great ones."

The decisive variable is leadership discipline, not feature depth.

8. Tool Governance as Leadership Work

Tool governance isn't clerical—it's cultural.

Leaders define:

- How information flows
- How decisions are made
- How accountability is shared

When leaders model disciplined use, teams follow.

Governance done right creates clarity, rhythm, and ownership.

9. Lessons from Elite Teams and Winning Cultures

- Bill Walsh: Systems > Scoreboard—clarity breeds consistency.
- Eric Schmidt & Bill Campbell: Coaching + structure drives innovation.
- Jocko Willink: Simplicity and discipline create adaptability.

Great teams win through clarity of system, not complexity of tools.

10. Lessons Learned

- Start with purpose, not features.

- Engage stakeholders early to define needs and workflows.
- Pilot before rollout to identify adoption barriers.
- Provide ongoing training and feedback.
- Lead from the front—when leaders use the system, others follow.
- Avoid shiny object syndrome—fit beats flash every time.

11. Key Themes

Theme	Summary
Purpose Before Platform	Begin with mission and stakeholder needs, not technology trends.
Right View = Right Decisions	Tailor information displays to support decision cadence.
Task-Technology Fit	Match functionality to actual work, not abstract features.
Evaluate Objectively	Use structured rubrics; test with real teams.
Discipline Drives Freedom	Simplicity and consistency accelerate agility.
Leadership Is the Decisive Variable	Tools succeed when leaders model adoption and clarity.
Governance = Leadership in Action	Information flow defines culture and accountability.

12. Memorable Quotes

- "The score takes care of itself." —Bill Walsh
- "Discipline equals freedom." —Jocko Willink
- "It's the people." —Bill Campbell
- "Leaders must own everything in their world." — Jocko Willink
- "The ability to concentrate and to use your time well is everything." —Lee Iacocca
- "Have the right conversations with the right people at the right time." —Eric Schmidt

13. Summary Insight

Technology should serve the mission, not define it.

When purpose drives selection and discipline governs use, tools become force multipliers—enhancing visibility, enabling more intelligent decisions, and sustaining trust across the organization.

Ultimately, clarity beats complexity, and leadership beats software.

NOTES

LEADING THE WORK

CHAPTER 18: MICRO-PIVOTS: PATTERNS FOR DAY-TO-DAY WINS

CORE IDEA

Big transformations get headlines; small, disciplined adjustments win the season.

Micro-pivots embed continuous improvement into daily rhythm—turning feedback into action without waiting for the next reorg.

1. Mindset of Continuous Improvement

- *Covey—Sharpen the Saw:* renew skills, systems, and relationships regularly.
- *Altucher—Small Bets:* test quickly, learn fast, scale what works.
- From "fix it next quarter" → "try it now, learn today."

2. Why Micro-Pivots Matter

- Speed: adjust in hours/days, not months.
- Lower Risk: small, reversible changes reduce blast radius.
- Learning Loops: frequent reflection accelerates insight.
- Cultural Signal: normalizes change; reduces fear.
- Compounding Gains: 5–10% monthly improvements $\rightarrow$ material performance lift.

3. Daily Practices (Plug-and-Play)

- Five-Slide Vision Deck (living): purpose, value, scope, milestones, risks; update biweekly.
- One-Page Status: deltas, blockers, decisions needed.
- Dependency Stand-Up (15 min/wk): what changed, what's blocking, who decides.
- Template Refresh (quarterly): retire friction, add what teams actually use.
- Risk Review Blitz (30 min/2 wks): close stale risks, reprioritize new ones.
- Learning Moments: end meetings with one insight / one improvement.

4. Agile as Micro-Pivot Engine

- Daily stand-ups: add "one small change I'll try today."
- Backlog refinement (weekly): reprioritize on fresh signal.
- Sprint retros: commit to one micro-pivot next sprint.

- Kanban tweaks: adjust WIP limits, swimlanes, pull rules mid-week.
- Demos & feedback: one micro-action per increment.

5. Real-World Signals

- Slack/Tiny Speck: internal tool iterated into product.
- Instagram/Burbn, YouTube: small, repeated adjustments guided by usage patterns.
- Lesson: observe → adjust small → observe again (MVP cycles).

6. Leadership Behaviors that Enable Micro-Pivots

- Model adaptability: "Thank you for trying—what did we learn?"
- Create safety: de-risk small experiments; praise early flags.
- Formalize rituals: daily/weekly/bi-weekly micro-pivot touchpoints.
- Broadcast micro-wins: make minor improvements visible and valued.
- *Walsh:* standards & systems → results.
- *Campbell:* "It's the people." Coaching > policing.
- *Willink:* Extreme Ownership—own what you can change now.

7. Practical Implementation Tips

- Start low-risk (meeting format, dashboard tweak).

- Co-create with the team: "What one thing would make next week easier?"
- Track impact: e.g., -15% prep time, -40% handoff delays, +20% throughput.
- Capture the pattern: what we tried → what happened → what's next.
- Use lightweight tools (Kanban, decision log, mini-dashboards).

8. Avoid These Pitfalls

- Over-tracking: don't turn micro-pivots into major projects.
- Change fatigue: keep cadence sustainable; rotate focus areas.
- No reflection: measure outcomes or stop doing it.
- Siloed tweaks: check cross-team impacts before changing flow.
- Culture drag: explain the "why," protect experimenters.

9. Embed the Rhythm (Project Economy)

- Explicit cadence: end-of-day check-ins, weekly stand-ups, biweekly risk blitz, monthly review.
- Visible improvement backlog: team-pull micro-pivots.
- Tie to metrics: latency, cycle time, blocker age, rework %, NPS/satisfaction.
- Close-out stories: "micro-pivot winners" at demos/all-hands.
- Onboard new teams into the habit.

10. Quick Metrics to Watch

- Cycle time/throughput (trend).
- Blocker age (target ↓).
- Dependency wait time (target ↓).
- Meeting load & prep time (target ↓).
- Defect leakage/rework (target ↓).
- Stakeholder satisfaction (target ↑).

11. One-Page Micro-Pivot Canvas (use anywhere)

- Problem (1–2 lines)
- Tiny change we'll try (this week)
- Owner & start date
- Expected effect & metric
- Check date & result
- Next action (adopt/adjust/drop)

12. Key Themes

- Small changes compound into a durable advantage.
- Agility lives in the day-to-day, not in annual plans.
- Leaders enable the habit—safety, standards, and visibility.
- Document & scale—turn wins into reusable patterns.
- Speed + safety = innovation without disruption.

13. Memorable Quotes

- "Sharpen the saw." —Stephen Covey

- "Iterate in small bets." —James Altucher
- "Discipline equals freedom." —Jocko Willink
- "The score will take care of itself." —Bill Walsh
- "The right conversations at the right time." —Bill Campbell
- "Small wins are the breadcrumbs of transformation." —Project Paradigm
- "In the project economy, the team that learns fastest wins." —Project Paradigm

14. Summary Insights

Micro-pivots are small, deliberate adjustments made daily to improve performance, foster learning, and maintain momentum. Rather than waiting for large transformations, teams adapt continuously—testing ideas, refining workflows, and scaling what works. These small shifts compound over time, building agility, reducing risk, and creating a culture of continuous improvement. In the project economy, where speed and adaptability define success, micro-pivots turn everyday work into a steady engine of progress.

CHAPTER 19: PROJECT MANAGEMENT TEMPLATE FORMS

NOTES

- Template Purpose and Standardization
  - Templates provide structural consistency across projects and serve as repeatable frameworks for planning, tracking, and governance. The NASA NAS PMO model was used as the practical foundation for this chapter.
- Charter and Scope Integration
  - The one-page Project Charter and Scope Statement reinforce Stephen Covey's "Begin with the End in Mind" principle—clarity of intent before execution.
- Communication and Visibility
  - The Communication Plan and One-Page Status Report align with Lee Iacocca's philosophy that "writing something down is the first step toward making it happen." Concise documentation strengthens accountability and transparency.

- Risk and Decision Management
  - Risk Registers and Decision Logs embody Kerzner's systems approach—linking uncertainty management to real-time decision traceability.
- Iterative Refinement
  - Regular updates to templates, such as quarterly refreshes or after-action lessons learned, reflect Altucher's notion of "iterating in small bets"— continuous improvement through small, fast feedback loops.
- Cultural Reinforcement
  - Consistent use of standard forms across projects cultivates shared understanding, reduces rework, and strengthens institutional memory—a concept echoed in Campbell's leadership coaching philosophy of clarity through communication.
- Adaptability Across Contexts
  - While developed in the NASA PMO environment, these templates can be scaled to fit academic, government, or private-sector projects with minimal modification.
- Digital Integration
  - Modern PMOs increasingly embed these templates within platforms such as Smartsheet, Confluence, or SharePoint to ensure live collaboration, version control, and data-driven decision-making.
- Closing Reflection
  - As Drucker emphasized, "What gets measured gets managed."
  - Templates are not bureaucratic paperwork—they are the frameworks that turn planning into progress and leadership into results.

CHAPTER 20

- Jordan B. Peterson's work is referenced primarily from *12 Rules for Life* and *Beyond Order*, emphasizing responsibility and meaning through voluntary challenge.
- Health insurance impacts are drawn from U.S. Bureau of Labor Statistics data and Kaiser Family Foundation trends on employer-based coverage.
- Concepts of projectization and family planning align with Stephen Covey's principles of proactivity and long-term vision from *The 7 Habits of Highly Effective People*.
- Economic and social commentary informed by insights from Drucker and Iacocca on individual responsibility and time management in changing work environments.

REFERENCES

BIBLIOGRAPHY

INTRODUCTION

- Branson, R. (2015). *The Virgin Way: Everything I Know About Leadership.* Portfolio.
- Bezos, J. (2017). *Shareholder Letters (1997–2017).* Amazon.com Inc.
- Schmidt, E., Rosenberg, J., & Eagle, A. (2019). *Trillion Dollar Coach: The Leadership Playbook of Silicon Valley's Bill Campbell.* Harper Business.
- Willink, J., & Babin, L. (2015). *Extreme Ownership: How U.S. Navy SEALs Lead and Win.* St. Martin's Press.
- Gibson, M. (2018). *Paper Belt on Fire: How Renegade Investors Sparked a Revolt Against the University.*
- Peterson, J. (2018). *12 Rules for Life: An Antidote to Chaos.*

CHAPTER 1

- Altucher, J. (2013). *Choose Yourself: Be Happy, Make Millions, Live the Dream.* Lioncrest Publishing.
- Covey, S. R. (1989). *The 7 Habits of Highly Effective People.* Free Press.
- Gibson, M. (2018). *Paper Belt on Fire: How Renegade Investors Sparked a Revolt Against the University.* PublicAffairs.
- Iacocca, L. (2007). *Where Have All the Leaders Gone?* Scribner.
- Iacocca, L. (1984). *Iacocca: An Autobiography.* Bantam Books.
- Kogon, K., Blakemore, S., & Wood, J. (2015). *Project Management for the Unofficial Project Manager.* BenBella Books.
- Standing, G. (2011). *The Precariat: The New Dangerous Class.* Bloomsbury Academic.
- Welch, J. & Byrne, J. A. (2001). *Jack: Straight from the Gut.* Warner Business Books.
- Microsoft. (2020). *Microsoft Teams Product Overview.* Microsoft Corporation.
- Slack Technologies. (2020). *Slack Product Documentation and Use Cases.* Slack Inc.

- Zoom Video Communications. (2020). *Zoom for Business Collaboration*. Zoom Video Communications.
- Asana. (2020). *Asana Project Management Platform*. Asana Inc.

CHAPTER 2

- Altucher, J. (2013). *Choose Yourself: Be Happy, Make Millions, Live the Dream*. Lioncrest Publishing.
- Covey, S. R. (1989). *The 7 Habits of Highly Effective People*. Free Press.
- Drucker, P. F. (1993). *Post-Capitalist Society*. HarperBusiness.
- Drucker, P. F. (2001). *The Essential Drucker: The Best of Sixty Years of Peter Drucker's Essential Writings on Management*. HarperBusiness.
- Iacocca, L. (2007). *Where Have All the Leaders Gone?* Scribner.
- Iacocca, L. (1984). *Iacocca: An Autobiography*. Bantam Books.
- Kogon, K., Blakemore, S., & Wood, J. (2015). *Project Management for the Unofficial Project Manager*. BenBella Books.
- Standing, G. (2011). *The Precariat: The New Dangerous Class*. Bloomsbury Academic.
- Welch, J. & Byrne, J. A. (2001). *Jack: Straight from the Gut*. Warner Business Books.
- Microsoft. (2020). *Microsoft Azure Documentation*. Microsoft Corporation.
- Amazon Web Services. (2020). *AWS Cloud Platform Overview*. Amazon.com Inc.
- Google Cloud. (2020). *Google Cloud Platform Documentation*. Google Inc.
- Zoom Video Communications. (2020). *Zoom for Business Collaboration*. Zoom Video Communications.
- Slack Technologies. (2020). *Slack Product Documentation and Use Cases*. Slack Inc.
- Trello (Atlassian). (2020). *Trello Product Documentation*. Atlassian Corporation.
- NASA Advanced Supercomputing Division. (2023). *NAS Project Management Office Guidelines and Templates*. NASA Ames Research Center.

CHAPTER 3

- Altucher, J. (2013). *Choose Yourself: Be Happy, Make Millions, Live the Dream.* Lioncrest Publishing.
- Covey, S. R. (1989). *The 7 Habits of Highly Effective People.* Free Press.
- Drucker, P. F. (1993). *Post-Capitalist Society.* HarperBusiness.
- Drucker, P. F. (2001). *The Essential Drucker: The Best of Sixty Years of Peter Drucker's Essential Writings on Management.* HarperBusiness.
- Iacocca, L. (2007). *Where Have All the Leaders Gone?* Scribner.
- Iacocca, L. (1984). *Iacocca: An Autobiography.* Bantam Books.
- Kogon, K., Blakemore, S., & Wood, J. (2015). *Project Management for the Unofficial Project Manager.* BenBella Books.
- Standing, G. (2011). *The Precariat: The New Dangerous Class.* Bloomsbury Academic.
- Welch, J. & Byrne, J. A. (2001). *Jack: Straight from the Gut.* Warner Business Books.

Labor Market and Freelance Economy

- Upwork. (2023). *Upwork Q4 2023 Earnings Report.* Upwork Inc.
- Fiverr International. (2023). *Fiverr Annual Report.* Fiverr International Ltd.
- Toptal. (2023). *Talent Network Overview.* Toptal LLC.
- World Economic Forum. (2023). *The Future of Jobs Report.* WEF.
- U.S. Bureau of Labor Statistics. (2023). *Contingent and Alternative Employment Arrangements Survey.* U.S. Department of Labor.

Technology Adoption & Tools

- Atlassian. (2023). *Jira Product Usage and Adoption Data.* Atlassian Corporation.
- Asana. (2023). *Asana Product Overview and Adoption Trends.* Asana Inc.
- Smartsheet. (2023). *Annual Report and Usage Metrics.* Smartsheet Inc.
- Trello (Atlassian). (2023). *Trello Product Documentation.* Atlassian Corporation.

- Monday.com. (2023). *Monday Work OS Usage and Growth Data.* Monday.com Ltd.
- Gartner. (2023). *Market Guide for Collaborative Work Management Platforms.* Gartner Inc.

Organizational Case Studies

- NASA Advanced Supercomputing Division. (2023). *NAS Project Management Office Guidelines and Results.* NASA Ames Research Center.
- U.S. General Services Administration. (2022). *Modernization and Agile Implementation Report.* GSA.
- Deloitte. (2023). *Global Human Capital Trends.* Deloitte Insights.
- McKinsey & Company. (2023). *The Project-Centric Organization: A New Operating Model.* McKinsey Global Institute.
- World Bank. (2022). *Public Sector Modernization through Project Portfolios.* World Bank Group.

Cultural and Workforce Trends

- Gallup. (2023). *State of the Global Workplace Report.* Gallup Inc.
- LinkedIn. (2023). *Global Talent Trends Report.* LinkedIn Corporation.
- Altucher, J. (2013). *Choose Yourself.* Lioncrest Publishing.
- Kogon, K. & Blakemore, S. (2015). *Project Management for the Unofficial Project Manager.* BenBella Books.

CHAPTER 4

- Altucher, J. (2013). *Choose Yourself: Be Happy, Make Millions, Live the Dream.* Lioncrest Publishing.
- Atlassian. (2023). *Agile Coach: Scrum, Kanban, and Agile Framework Resources.* Atlassian Corporation.
- Beck, K. et al. (2001). *Manifesto for Agile Software Development.* Agile Alliance.
- Covey, S. R. (1989). *The 7 Habits of Highly Effective People.* Free Press.
- Ford, H. (1922). *My Life and Work.* Garden City Publishing.
- Highsmith, J. (2002). *Agile Software Development Ecosystems.* Addison-Wesley.

- Iacocca, L. (2007). *Where Have All the Leaders Gone?* Scribner.
- Iacocca, L. (1984). *Iacocca: An Autobiography*. Bantam Books.
- Kogon, K., Blakemore, S., & Wood, J. (2015). *Project Management for the Unofficial Project Manager*. BenBella Books.
- PMI (Project Management Institute). (2021). *A Guide to the Project Management Body of Knowledge (PMBOK® Guide) – Seventh Edition*. Project Management Institute.
- PMI. (2017). *Agile Practice Guide*. Project Management Institute.
- Sutherland, J. (2014). *Scrum: The Art of Doing Twice the Work in Half the Time*. Crown Business.
- Tuckman, B. W. (1965). "Developmental Sequence in Small Groups." *Psychological Bulletin, 63(6), 384–399.*
- Tuckman, B. W., & Jensen, M. A. C. (1977). "Stages of Small-Group Development Revisited." *Group & Organization Studies, 2(4), 419–427.*
- Womack, J. P., & Jones, D. T. (2003). *Lean Thinking: Banish Waste and Create Wealth in Your Corporation*. Free Press.
- NASA Advanced Supercomputing Division. (2023). *NAS PMO Hybrid Project Management Practices and Guidelines*. NASA Ames Research Center.
- Jack Welch & Byrne, J. A. (2001). *Jack: Straight from the Gut*. Warner Business Books.

CHAPTER 5

- Altucher, J. (2013). *Choose Yourself: Be Happy, Make Millions, Live the Dream*. Lioncrest Publishing.
- Covey, S. R. (1989). *The 7 Habits of Highly Effective People*. Free Press.
- Drucker, P. F. (1993). *Post-Capitalist Society*. HarperBusiness.
- Drucker, P. F. (2001). *The Essential Drucker: The Best of Sixty Years of Peter Drucker's Essential Writings on Management*. HarperBusiness.
- Gantt, H. L. (1919). *Organizing for Work*. Harcourt, Brace & Howe.
- Gantt, H. L. (1910). *Work, Wages, and Profits*. The Engineering Magazine Company.
- Iacocca, L. (1984). *Iacocca: An Autobiography*. Bantam Books.
- Iacocca, L. (2007). *Where Have All the Leaders Gone?* Scribner.
- Kogon, K., Blakemore, S., & Wood, J. (2015). *Project Management for the Unofficial Project Manager*. BenBella Books.

- PMI (Project Management Institute). (2021). *A Guide to the Project Management Body of Knowledge (PMBOK® Guide) – Seventh Edition*. Project Management Institute.
- PMI. (2017). *Agile Practice Guide*. Project Management Institute.
- Welch, J. & Byrne, J. A. (2001). *Jack: Straight from the Gut*. Warner Business Books.
- NASA Advanced Supercomputing Division. (2023). *NAS PMO Charter Templates and Governance Framework*. NASA Ames Research Center.
- Atlassian. (2023). *Project Charter Best Practices Guide*. Atlassian Corporation.
- Smartsheet Inc. (2022). *Project Charter Templates and Use Cases*. Smartsheet Inc.
- Harvard Business Review. (2016). "Why Project Charters Matter More Than Ever." *Harvard Business Review*.
- Deloitte. (2022). *The Project-Driven Organization: Aligning Strategy and Execution*. Deloitte Insights.

CHAPTER 6

- Altucher, J. (2013). *Choose Yourself: Be Happy, Make Millions, Live the Dream*. Lioncrest Publishing.
- Covey, S. R. (1989). *The 7 Habits of Highly Effective People*. Free Press.
- Drucker, P. F. (1993). *Post-Capitalist Society*. HarperBusiness.
- Drucker, P. F. (2001). *The Essential Drucker: The Best of Sixty Years of Peter Drucker's Essential Writings on Management*. HarperBusiness.
- Gantt, H. L. (1919). *Organizing for Work*. Harcourt, Brace & Howe.
- Gantt, H. L. (1910). *Work, Wages, and Profits*. The Engineering Magazine Company.
- Iacocca, L. (1984). *Iacocca: An Autobiography*. Bantam Books.
- Iacocca, L. (2007). *Where Have All the Leaders Gone?* Scribner.
- Kogon, K., Blakemore, S., & Wood, J. (2015). *Project Management for the Unofficial Project Manager*. BenBella Books.
- Walsh, B. (2009). *The Score Takes Care of Itself: My Philosophy of Leadership*. Portfolio.
- Welch, J. & Byrne, J. A. (2001). *Jack: Straight from the Gut*. Warner Business Books.

- NASA Advanced Supercomputing Division. (2023). *NAS PMO Communication Templates and Portfolio Review Guidelines*. NASA Ames Research Center.
- Atlassian. (2023). *Project Communication Best Practices*. Atlassian Corporation.
- Slack Technologies. (2023). *Slack for Teams: Communication and Collaboration*. Slack Inc.
- Zoom Video Communications. (2023). *Zoom Meeting Effectiveness Guide*. Zoom Video Communications.
- Smartsheet Inc. (2023). *Project Status Reporting and Communication Templates*. Smartsheet Inc.
- Gallup. (2022). *State of the Global Workplace Report*. Gallup Inc.
- Harvard Business Review. (2013). "The Hidden Power of Effective Communication in Organizations." *Harvard Business Review*.
- McKinsey & Company. (2020). *How Clear Communication Accelerates Transformation*. McKinsey Global Institute.
- Deloitte. (2022). *The Project-Driven Organization: Communication as an Enabler of Agility*. Deloitte Insights.

CHAPTER 7

- Covey, S. R. (1989). *The 7 Habits of Highly Effective People*. Free Press.
- Drucker, P. F. (1993). *Post-Capitalist Society*. HarperBusiness.
- Drucker, P. F. (2001). *The Essential Drucker: The Best of Sixty Years of Peter Drucker's Essential Writings on Management*. HarperBusiness.
- Iacocca, L. (1984). *Iacocca: An Autobiography*. Bantam Books.
- Iacocca, L. (2007). *Where Have All the Leaders Gone?* Scribner.
- Kogon, K., Blakemore, S., & Wood, J. (2015). *Project Management for the Unofficial Project Manager*. BenBella Books.
- PMI (Project Management Institute). (2021). *A Guide to the Project Management Body of Knowledge (PMBOK® Guide) – Seventh Edition*. Project Management Institute.
- PMI. (2017). *Agile Practice Guide*. Project Management Institute.
- NASA Advanced Supercomputing Division. (2023). *NAS Project Management Office Implementation Report*. NASA Ames Research Center.
- NASA HECC Program. (2023). *High-End Computing Capability Strategic Priorities*. NASA Ames Research Center.

- NASA Office of the Chief Information Officer. (2022). *NASA Program and Project Management (NPR 7120.5)*. NASA Headquarters.
- McKinsey & Company. (2023). *Modern PMOs: How Lightweight Governance Accelerates Impact*. McKinsey Global Institute.
- Deloitte. (2022). *The Adaptive PMO: Driving Business Value Through Portfolio Agility*. Deloitte Insights.
- Gartner. (2023). *Evolving PMO Functions in High-Complexity Environments*. Gartner Inc.
- Government Accountability Office (GAO). (2022). *Best Practices for Project and Program Management in Federal Agencies*. U.S. GAO.
- Altucher, J. (2013). *Choose Yourself: Be Happy, Make Millions, Live the Dream*. Lioncrest Publishing.
- Walsh, B. (2009). *The Score Takes Care of Itself: My Philosophy of Leadership*. Portfolio.
- Welch, J. & Byrne, J. A. (2001). *Jack: Straight from the Gut*. Warner Business Books.

CHAPTER 8

- Altucher, J. (2013). Choose Yourself: *Be Happy, Make Millions, Live the Dream*. Lioncrest Publishing.
- Covey, S. R. (1989). *The 7 Habits of Highly Effective People*. Free Press.
- Drucker, P. F. (1993). *Post-Capitalist Society*. HarperBusiness.
- Drucker, P. F. (2001). *The Essential Drucker: The Best of Sixty Years of Peter Drucker's Essential Writings on Management*. HarperBusiness.
- Iacocca, L. (1984). *Iacocca: An Autobiography*. Bantam Books.
- Iacocca, L. (2007). *Where Have All the Leaders Gone?* Scribner.
- Kogon, K., Blakemore, S., & Wood, J. (2015). *Project Management for the Unofficial Project Manager*. BenBella Books.
- PMI (Project Management Institute). (2021). *A Guide to the Project Management Body of Knowledge (PMBOK® Guide) – Seventh Edition*. Project Management Institute.
- PMI. (2017). *Agile Practice Guide*. Project Management Institute.
- NASA Advanced Supercomputing Division. (2023). *NAS PMO Governance and Change Control Framework*. NASA Ames Research Center.

- NASA HECC Program. (2023). *High-End Computing Capability Strategic Priorities*. NASA Ames Research Center.
- NASA Office of the Chief Information Officer. (2022). *NASA Program and Project Management Requirements (NPR 7120.5)*. NASA Headquarters.
- Government Accountability Office (GAO). (2022). *Best Practices for Project and Program Management in Federal Agencies*. U.S. GAO.
- McKinsey & Company. (2023). *Evolving PMO Governance for Speed and Control*. McKinsey Global Institute.
- Deloitte. (2022). *The Adaptive PMO: Governance That Enables Agility*. Deloitte Insights.
- Gartner. (2023). *Modern PMO Structures and Governance Models*. Gartner Inc.
- Harvard Business Review. (2019). "How Governance Models Accelerate Project Delivery." *Harvard Business Review*.

CHAPTER 9

- Altucher, J. (2013). *Choose Yourself: Be Happy, Make Millions, Live the Dream*. Lioncrest Publishing.
- Covey, S. R. (1989). *The 7 Habits of Highly Effective People*. Free Press.
- Drucker, P. F. (1993*). Post-Capitalist Society*. HarperBusiness.
- Drucker, P. F. (2001). *The Essential Drucker: The Best of Sixty Years of Peter Drucker's Essential Writings on Management*. HarperBusiness.
- Gantt, H. L. (1919). *Organizing for Work*. Harcourt, Brace & Howe.
- Gantt, H. L. (1910). *Work, Wages, and Profits*. The Engineering Magazine Company.
- Iacocca, L. (1984). *Iacocca: An Autobiography*. Bantam Books.
- Iacocca, L. (2007). *Where Have All the Leaders Gone?* Scribner.
- Kogon, K., Blakemore, S., & Wood, J. (2015). *Project Management for the Unofficial Project Manager*. BenBella Books.
- PMI (Project Management Institute). (2021). *A Guide to the Project Management Body of Knowledge (PMBOK® Guide) – Seventh Edition*. Project Management Institute.
- PMI. (2017). *Agile Practice Guide*. Project Management Institute.
- NASA Advanced Supercomputing Division. (2023). *NAS PMO*

Performance Measurement and Lessons Learned Report. NASA Ames Research Center.

- NASA HECC Program. (2023). *High-End Computing Capability Strategic Priorities*. NASA Ames Research Center.
- NASA Office of the Chief Information Officer. (2022). *NASA Program and Project Management Requirements (NPR 7120.5)*. NASA Headquarters.
- Government Accountability Office (GAO). (2022). *Best Practices for Project and Program Management in Federal Agencies*. U.S. GAO.
- Deloitte. (2022). *Measuring What Matters: How Modern PMOs Use Data for Strategic Decisions*. Deloitte Insights.
- McKinsey & Company. (2023). *PMO Impact: Linking Metrics to Culture and Performance*. McKinsey Global Institute.
- Gartner. (2023). *PMO Metrics and Cultural Change: Enabling Organizational Agility*. Gartner Inc.
- Harvard Business Review. (2019). "How Great Leaders Build Feedback Loops that Drive Change." *Harvard Business Review*.
- Kotter, J. P. (1996). *Leading Change*. Harvard Business School Press.
- Schein, E. H. (2017). *Organizational Culture and Leadership* (5th ed.). Wiley.
- Cameron, K. S., & Quinn, R. E. (2011). *Diagnosing and Changing Organizational Culture: Based on the Competing Values Framework*. Jossey-Bass.
- Prosci. (2022). *Best Practices in Change Management Benchmarking Report*. Prosci Inc.

CHAPTER 10

- Altucher, J. (2013). *Choose Yourself: Be Happy, Make Millions, Live the Dream*. Lioncrest Publishing.
- Covey, S. R. (1989). *The 7 Habits of Highly Effective People*. Free Press.
- Drucker, P. F. (1993). *Post-Capitalist Society*. HarperBusiness.
- Drucker, P. F. (2001). *The Essential Drucker: The Best of Sixty Years of Peter Drucker's Essential Writings on Management*. HarperBusiness.
- Drucker, P. F. (1995). *Managing in a Time of Great Change*. Butterworth-Heinemann.
- Iacocca, L. (1984). *Iacocca: An Autobiography*. Bantam Books.

- Iacocca, L. (2007). *Where Have All the Leaders Gone?* Scribner.
- Kogon, K., Blakemore, S., & Wood, J. (2015). *Project Management for the Unofficial Project Manager*. BenBella Books.
- PMI (Project Management Institute). (2021). *A Guide to the Project Management Body of Knowledge (PMBOK® Guide) – Seventh Edition*. Project Management Institute.
- PMI. (2017). *Agile Practice Guide*. Project Management Institute.
- NASA Office of the Chief Information Officer. (2022). *NASA Program and Project Management Requirements (NPR 7120.5)*. NASA Headquarters.
- NASA Advanced Supercomputing Division. (2023). *NAS PMO Ethics and Governance Engagement Practices*. NASA Ames Research Center.
- GAO (U.S. Government Accountability Office). (2022). *Best Practices for Project and Program Management in Federal Agencies*. U.S. GAO.
- Prosci. (2022). *Best Practices in Change Management Benchmarking Report*. Prosci Inc.
- Kotter, J. P. (1996). *Leading Change*. Harvard Business School Press.
- Schein, E. H. (2017). *Organizational Culture and Leadership* (5th ed.). Wiley.
- Cameron, K. S., & Quinn, R. E. (2011). *Diagnosing and Changing Organizational Culture: Based on the Competing Values Framework*. Jossey-Bass.
- Harvard Business Review. (2019). "Why Fair Process Matters in Organizational Change." *Harvard Business Review*.
- Brown, B. (2018). *Dare to Lead: Brave Work. Tough Conversations. Whole Hearts*. Random House.
- Edmondson, A. C. (2019). *The Fearless Organization: Creating Psychological Safety in the Workplace for Learning, Innovation, and Growth*. Wiley.
- Deloitte. (2022). *Ethical Leadership and Organizational Agility*. Deloitte Insights.
- McKinsey & Company. (2023). *Human-Centered Transformation: The Ethical Edge in Change Management*. McKinsey Global Institute.
- Gartner. (2023). *Ethics, Trust, and Governance in PMO Transformations*. Gartner Inc.

CHAPTER 11

- Altucher, J. (2013). *Choose Yourself: Be Happy, Make Millions, Live the Dream.* Lioncrest Publishing.
- Brown, B. (2018). *Dare to Lead: Brave Work. Tough Conversations. Whole Hearts.* Random House.
- Covey, S. R. (1989). *The 7 Habits of Highly Effective People.* Free Press.
- Drucker, P. F. (1993). *Post-Capitalist Society.* HarperBusiness.
- Drucker, P. F. (2001). *The Essential Drucker: The Best of Sixty Years of Peter Drucker's Essential Writings on Management.* HarperBusiness.
- Edmondson, A. C. (2019). *The Fearless Organization: Creating Psychological Safety in the Workplace for Learning, Innovation, and Growth.* Wiley.
- Gantt, H. L. (1910). *Work, Wages, and Profits.* The Engineering Magazine Company.
- Gantt, H. L. (1919). *Organizing for Work.* Harcourt, Brace & Howe.
- Iacocca, L. (1984). *Iacocca: An Autobiography.* Bantam Books.
- Iacocca, L. (2007). *Where Have All the Leaders Gone?* Scribner.
- Kogon, K., Blakemore, S., & Wood, J. (2015). *Project Management for the Unofficial Project Manager.* BenBella Books.
- Kotter, J. P. (1996). *Leading Change.* Harvard Business School Press.
- McKinsey & Company. (2023). *The New Leadership Playbook: Building Teams That Adapt and Perform.* McKinsey Global Institute.
- PMI (Project Management Institute). (2021). *A Guide to the Project Management Body of Knowledge (PMBOK® Guide) – Seventh Edition.* Project Management Institute.
- PMI. (2017). *Agile Practice Guide.* Project Management Institute.
- Schein, E. H. (2017). *Organizational Culture and Leadership* (5th ed.). Wiley.
- Tuckman, B. W. (1965). "Developmental Sequence in Small Groups." *Psychological Bulletin, 63(6), 384–399.*
- Tuckman, B. W., & Jensen, M. A. C. (1977). "Stages of Small-Group Development Revisited." *Group & Organization Studies, 2(4), 419–427.*
- Welch, J. (2001). *Jack: Straight from the Gut.* Warner Business Books.

- Harvard Business Review. (2020). "What Great Project Leaders Do Differently." *Harvard Business Review.*
- Deloitte. (2022). *Leadership in High-Performance Teams: Patterns of Effective Execution.* Deloitte Insights.
- Gartner. (2023). *Leadership Competencies for Project-Driven Organizations.* Gartner Inc.
- NASA Advanced Supercomputing Division. (2023). *NAS PMO Leadership Practices and Team Development Guidelines.* NASA Ames Research Center.

CHAPTER 12

- Altucher, J. (2013). *Choose Yourself: Be Happy, Make Millions, Live the Dream.* Lioncrest Publishing.
- Brown, B. (2018). *Dare to Lead: Brave Work. Tough Conversations.* Whole Hearts. Random House.
- Campbell, E., Schmidt, E., Rosenberg, J., & Eagle, A. (2019). *Trillion Dollar Coach: The Leadership Playbook of Silicon Valley's Bill Campbell.* Harper Business.
- Covey, S. R. (1989). *The 7 Habits of Highly Effective People.* Free Press.
- Drucker, P. F. (1993). *Post-Capitalist Society.* HarperBusiness.
- Drucker, P. F. (2001). *The Essential Drucker: The Best of Sixty Years of Peter Drucker's Essential Writings on Management.* HarperBusiness.
- Edmondson, A. C. (2019). *The Fearless Organization: Creating Psychological Safety in the Workplace for Learning, Innovation, and Growth.* Wiley.
- Gantt, H. L. (1919). *Organizing for Work.* Harcourt, Brace & Howe.
- Iacocca, L. (1984). *Iacocca: An Autobiography.* Bantam Books.
- Iacocca, L. (2007). *Where Have All the Leaders Gone?* Scribner.
- Kogon, K., Blakemore, S., & Wood, J. (2015). *Project Management for the Unofficial Project Manager.* BenBella Books.
- Kotter, J. P. (1996). *Leading Change.* Harvard Business School Press.
- Schein, E. H. (2017). *Organizational Culture and Leadership* (5th ed.). Wiley.
- Cameron, K. S., & Quinn, R. E. (2011). *Diagnosing and Changing Organizational Culture: Based on the Competing Values Framework.* Jossey-Bass.

- PMI (Project Management Institute). (2021). *A Guide to the Project Management Body of Knowledge (PMBOK® Guide) – Seventh Edition*. Project Management Institute.
- PMI. (2017). *Agile Practice Guide*. Project Management Institute.
- NASA Advanced Supercomputing Division. (2023). *Knowledge Capture and Documentation Standards*. NASA Ames Research Center.
- NASA Office of the Chief Information Officer. (2022). *NASA Program and Project Management Requirements (NPR 7120.5)*. NASA Headquarters.
- Harvard Business Review. (2018). "Psychological Safety and the Crucial Role of Leadership." *Harvard Business Review*.
- Deloitte. (2022). *Culture by Design: Building Organizational Resilience*. Deloitte Insights.
- McKinsey & Company. (2023). *The Culture Factor in Transformation*. McKinsey Global Institute.
- Gartner. (2023). *Knowledge Management and Cultural Enablers in Projectized Organizations*. Gartner Inc.
- Prosci. (2022). *Best Practices in Change Management Benchmarking Report*. Prosci Inc.
- Welch, J. (2001). *Jack: Straight from the Gut*. Warner Business Books.

CHAPTER 13

- Altucher, J. (2013). *Choose Yourself: Be Happy, Make Millions, Live the Dream*. Lioncrest Publishing.
- Covey, S. R. (1989). *The 7 Habits of Highly Effective People*. Free Press.
- Drucker, P. F. (1993). *Post-Capitalist Society*. HarperBusiness.
- Drucker, P. F. (2001). *The Essential Drucker: The Best of Sixty Years of Peter Drucker's Essential Writings on Management*. HarperBusiness.
- Iacocca, L. (1984). *Iacocca: An Autobiography*. Bantam Books.
- Iacocca, L. (2007). *Where Have All the Leaders Gone?* Scribner.
- PMI (Project Management Institute). (2021). *A Guide to the Project Management Body of Knowledge (PMBOK® Guide) – Seventh Edition*. Project Management Institute.
- PMI. (2017). *Agile Practice Guide*. Project Management Institute.
- Kerzner, H. (2017). *Project Management: A Systems Approach to Planning, Scheduling, and Controlling* (12th ed.). Wiley.

- Lock, D. (2020). *Project Management* (11th ed.). Routledge.
- Meredith, J. R., Shafer, S. M., & Mantel, S. J. (2017). *Project Management: A Managerial Approach* (10th ed.). Wiley.
- Gantt, H. L. (1910). *Work, Wages, and Profits.* The Engineering Magazine Company.
- Gantt, H. L. (1919). *Organizing for Work.* Harcourt, Brace & Howe.
- Goldratt, E. M. (1997). *Critical Chain.* The North River Press.
- Leach, L. P. (2014). *Critical Chain Project Management* (3rd ed.). Artech House.
- NASA Office of the Chief Information Officer. (2022). *NASA Program and Project Management Requirements (NPR 7120.5).* NASA Headquarters.
- NASA Advanced Supercomputing Division. (2023). *NAS PMO Scheduling and Variance Management Guidelines.* NASA Ames Research Center.
- Project Management Institute. (2014). *Practice Standard for Scheduling – Second Edition.* PMI.
- Weber, R. (2020). *Scheduling and Cost Control for Engineering and Construction Projects.* Wiley.
- Harvard Business Review. (2020). "Why Realistic Scheduling Is a Leadership Imperative." *Harvard Business Review.*
- Deloitte. (2022). *Execution Under Uncertainty: Scheduling and Forecasting Best Practices.* Deloitte Insights.
- McKinsey & Company. (2023). *The Execution Advantage: How Realistic Forecasting Improves Delivery.* McKinsey Global Institute.
- Gartner. (2023). *Forecasting and Schedule Control in High-Complexity Projects.* Gartner Inc.
- Prosci. (2022). *Best Practices in Change Management Benchmarking Report.* Prosci Inc.

CHAPTER 14

- Altucher, J. (2013). *Choose Yourself: Be Happy, Make Millions, Live the Dream.* Lioncrest Publishing.
- Covey, S. R. (1989). *The 7 Habits of Highly Effective People.* Free Press.
- Drucker, P. F. (2001). *The Essential Drucker: The Best of Sixty Years of Peter Drucker's Essential Writings on Management.* HarperBusiness.

- Gantt, H. L. (1919). *Organizing for Work.* Harcourt, Brace & Howe.
- Goldratt, E. M. (1997). *Critical Chain.* North River Press.
- Hillson, D. (2009). *Managing Risk in Projects.* Gower Publishing.
- Iacocca, L. (1984). *Iacocca: An Autobiography.* Bantam Books.
- Iacocca, L. (2007). *Where Have All the Leaders Gone?* Scribner.
- Kerzner, H. (2017). *Project Management: A Systems Approach to Planning, Scheduling, and Controlling* (12th ed.). Wiley.
- Kendrick, T. (2015). *Identifying and Managing Project Risk: Essential Tools for Failure-Proofing Your Project.* AMACOM.
- Leach, L. P. (2014). *Critical Chain Project Management* (3rd ed.). Artech House.
- Meredith, J. R., Shafer, S. M., & Mantel, S. J. (2017). *Project Management: A Managerial Approach* (10th ed.). Wiley.
- PMI (Project Management Institute). (2021). *A Guide to the Project Management Body of Knowledge (PMBOK® Guide) – Seventh Edition.* Project Management Institute.
- PMI. (2019). *Practice Standard for Project Risk Management.* Project Management Institute.
- PMI. (2014). *Practice Standard for Scheduling – Second Edition.* Project Management Institute.
- SPMBOK (2020). *The Standard for Risk Management in Portfolios, Programs, and Projects.* Project Management Institute.
- NASA Office of the Chief Information Officer. (2022). *NASA Program and Project Management Requirements (NPR 7120.5).* NASA Headquarters.
- NASA Advanced Supercomputing Division. (2023). *NAS PMO Risk & Dependency Management Guidelines.* NASA Ames Research Center.
- Deloitte. (2022). *Managing Interdependencies in Complex Programs.* Deloitte Insights.
- McKinsey & Company. (2023). *The Risk Advantage: How Proactive Dependency Management Improves Delivery.* McKinsey Global Institute.
- Gartner. (2023). *Risk, Dependency, and Resilience in Modern Project Portfolios.* Gartner Inc.
- Harvard Business Review. (2021). "Why Small Risks Become Big Problems." *Harvard Business Review.*
- Prosci. (2022). *Best Practices in Change Management Benchmarking Report.* Prosci Inc.

- Ward, S., & Chapman, C. (2003). *Project Risk Management: Processes, Techniques and Insights.* Wiley.

CHAPTER 15

- Altucher, J. (2013). *Choose Yourself: Be Happy, Make Millions, Live the Dream.* Lioncrest Publishing.
- Brynjolfsson, E., & McAfee, A. (2014). *The Second Machine Age: Work, Progress, and Prosperity in a Time of Brilliant Technologies.* W. W. Norton & Company.
- Brynjolfsson, E., Rock, D., & Syverson, C. (2018). "Artificial Intelligence and the Modern Productivity Paradox." *NBER Working Paper Series.*
- Campbell, E., Schmidt, E., Rosenberg, J., & Eagle, A. (2019). *Trillion Dollar Coach: The Leadership Playbook of Silicon Valley's Bill Campbell.* Harper Business.
- Covey, S. R. (1989). *The 7 Habits of Highly Effective People.* Free Press.
- Davenport, T. H., & Ronanki, R. (2018). "Artificial Intelligence for the Real World." *Harvard Business Review.*
- Davenport, T. H., & Kirby, J. (2016). *Only Humans Need Apply: Winners and Losers in the Age of Smart Machines.* Harper Business.
- Drucker, P. F. (2001). *The Essential Drucker.* HarperBusiness.
- Gartner. (2023). *AI in Project and Portfolio Management: Adoption, Governance, and Risk Mitigation.* Gartner Inc.
- Goldratt, E. M. (1997). *Critical Chain.* North River Press.
- Iacocca, L. (1984). *Iacocca: An Autobiography.* Bantam Books.
- Iacocca, L. (2007). *Where Have All the Leaders Gone?* Scribner.
- Kerzner, H. (2022). *Innovation Project Management.* Wiley.
- Kerzner, H. (2017). *Project Management: A Systems Approach to Planning, Scheduling, and Controlling* (12th ed.). Wiley.
- Leach, L. P. (2014). *Critical Chain Project Management* (3rd ed.). Artech House.
- Meredith, J. R., Shafer, S. M., & Mantel, S. J. (2017). *Project Management: A Managerial Approach* (10th ed.). Wiley.
- PMI (Project Management Institute). (2021). *A Guide to the Project Management Body of Knowledge (PMBOK® Guide) – Seventh Edition.* Project Management Institute.
- PMI. (2023). *AI and the Future of Project Management: Global Megatrends Report.* Project Management Institute.

- PwC. (2022). *AI in the Project Economy: From Augmentation to Acceleration.* PwC Insights.
- Deloitte. (2023). *AI and Automation in Program Delivery.* Deloitte Insights.
- McKinsey & Company. (2023). *Rewired: The Playbook for Digital Transformation.* McKinsey Global Institute.
- McKinsey & Company. (2022). *The State of AI: Shifting from Experimentation to Adoption.*
- Microsoft Research. (2023). *AI-Powered Predictive Scheduling and Workforce Planning.*
- Prosci. (2022). *Best Practices in Change Management Benchmarking Report.* Prosci Inc.
- Russell, S., & Norvig, P. (2020). *Artificial Intelligence: A Modern Approach* (4th ed.). Pearson.
- Tapscott, D., & Tapscott, A. (2016). *Blockchain Revolution.* Penguin.
- Welch, J. (2001). *Jack: Straight from the Gut.* Warner Business Books.
- WEF (World Economic Forum). (2023). *The Future of Jobs Report.* World Economic Forum.

CHAPTER 16

- Altucher, J. (2013). *Choose Yourself: Be Happy, Make Millions, Live the Dream.* Lioncrest Publishing.
- Covey, S. R. (1989). *The 7 Habits of Highly Effective People.* Free Press.
- Drucker, P. F. (2001). *The Essential Drucker.* HarperBusiness.
- Gartner. (2023). *Establishing a High-Impact PMO: Governance, Agility, and Business Value.* Gartner Inc.
- Goldratt, E. M. (1997). *Critical Chain.* North River Press.
- Hill, G. M. (2008). *The Complete Project Management Office Handbook (2nd ed.).* Auerbach Publications.
- Iacocca, L. (2007). *Where Have All the Leaders Gone?* Scribner.
- Iacocca, L. (1984). *Iacocca: An Autobiography.* Bantam Books.
- Kerzner, H. (2017). *Project Management: A Systems Approach to Planning, Scheduling, and Controlling* (12th ed.). Wiley.
- Kerzner, H. (2019). *Using the Project Management Maturity Model: Strategic Planning for Project Management* (3rd ed.). Wiley.

- Kogon, K., Blakemore, S., & Wood, J. (2015). *Project Management for the Unofficial Project Manager*. BenBella Books.
- Kendrick, T. (2015). *Identifying and Managing Project Risk: Essential Tools for Failure-Proofing Your Project*. AMACOM.
- Leach, L. P. (2014). *Critical Chain Project Management* (3rd ed.). Artech House.
- McKinsey & Company. (2023). *The Next Generation PMO: From Control Tower to Value Creator*. McKinsey Global Institute.
- Meredith, J. R., Shafer, S. M., & Mantel, S. J. (2017). *Project Management: A Managerial Approach* (10th ed.). Wiley.
- NASA Advanced Supercomputing Division. (2023). *NAS PMO and CCB Operating Procedures*. NASA Ames Research Center.
- NASA Office of the Chief Information Officer. (2022). *NASA Program and Project Management Requirements (NPR 7120.5)*. NASA Headquarters.
- PMI (Project Management Institute). (2021). *A Guide to the Project Management Body of Knowledge (PMBOK® Guide) – Seventh Edition*. Project Management Institute.
- PMI. (2017). *Agile Practice Guide*. Project Management Institute.
- PMI. (2013). *The Standard for Portfolio Management* (3rd ed.). Project Management Institute.
- Prosci. (2022). *Best Practices in Change Management Benchmarking Report*. Prosci Inc.
- Project Management Institute. (2013). *The Standard for Program Management* (3rd ed.). PMI.
- Steve Jobs quoted in: Isaacson, W. (2011). *Steve Jobs*. Simon & Schuster.
- Ward, J. L., & Daniel, E. M. (2012). *Benefits Management: How to Increase the Business Value of Your IT Projects* (2nd ed.). Wiley.
- Harvard Business Review. (2020). "Why PMOs Fail — and How to Make Yours Succeed." *Harvard Business Review*.
- Deloitte. (2023). *Building Adaptive PMOs: Driving Change and Innovation*. Deloitte Insights.
- PwC. (2023). *PMO Transformation Report: Building Strategic Delivery Engines*. PwC Insights.

CHAPTER 17

- Altucher, J. (2013). *Choose Yourself: Be Happy, Make Millions, Live the Dream*. Lioncrest Publishing.

- Campbell, E., Schmidt, E., Rosenberg, J., & Eagle, A. (2019). *Trillion Dollar Coach: The Leadership Playbook of Silicon Valley's Bill Campbell*. Harper Business.
- Covey, S. R. (1989). *The 7 Habits of Highly Effective People*. Free Press.
- Drucker, P. F. (2001). *The Essential Drucker*. HarperBusiness.
- Gartner. (2023). *Strategic PMO Technology Selection and Tool Alignment Framework*. Gartner Inc.
- Goldratt, E. M. (1997). *Critical Chain*. North River Press.
- Iacocca, L. (1984). *Iacocca: An Autobiography*. Bantam Books.
- Iacocca, L. (2007). *Where Have All the Leaders Gone?* Scribner.
- Jocko Willink & Babin, L. (2015). *Extreme Ownership: How U.S. Navy SEALs Lead and Win*. St. Martin's Press.
- Kerzner, H. (2017). Project Management: *A Systems Approach to Planning, Scheduling, and Controlling* (12th ed.). Wiley.
- Kerzner, H. (2019). *Innovation Project Management*. Wiley.
- Kogon, K., Blakemore, S., & Wood, J. (2015). *Project Management for the Unofficial Project Manager*. BenBella Books.
- McKinsey & Company. (2023). *Digital Transformation and Tool Fit in Project Organizations*. McKinsey Global Institute.
- Meredith, J. R., Shafer, S. M., & Mantel, S. J. (2017). *Project Management: A Managerial Approach* (10th ed.). Wiley.
- NASA Advanced Supercomputing Division. (2023). *Tool Evaluation and Integration Framework*. NASA Ames Research Center.
- PMI (Project Management Institute). (2021). *A Guide to the Project Management Body of Knowledge (PMBOK® Guide) – Seventh Edition*. Project Management Institute.
- PMI. (2017). *Agile Practice Guide*. Project Management Institute.
- Prosci. (2022). *Best Practices in Change Management Benchmarking Report*. Prosci Inc.
- Walsh, B. (2009). *The Score Takes Care of Itself: My Philosophy of Leadership*. Portfolio.
- Deloitte. (2023). *Technology Enablement and PMO Excellence*. Deloitte Insights.
- PwC. (2023). *Digital PMO Transformation Report*. PwC Insights.
- Harvard Business Review. (2022). "How to Choose the Right Technology for Your Organization." *Harvard Business Review*.
- MIT Sloan Management Review. (2021). "Tool Fit Over Trend:

Digital Alignment in High-Performance Organizations." *MIT Sloan Management Review*.

- Gartner. (2022). *Avoiding "Shiny Object" Syndrome in PM Technology Adoption*. Gartner Inc.
- McChrystal, S. (2015). *Team of Teams: New Rules of Engagement for a Complex World*. Penguin.
- Altucher, J. (2014). *The Choose Yourself Guide to Wealth*. Lioncrest Publishing.

CHAPTER 18

- Altucher, J. (2013). *Choose Yourself: Be Happy, Make Millions, Live the Dream*. Lioncrest Publishing.
- Altucher, J. (2014). *The Choose Yourself Guide to Wealth*. Lioncrest Publishing.
- Beck, K., et al. (2001). *Manifesto for Agile Software Development*. Agile Alliance.
- Beck, K. (2005). *Extreme Programming Explained: Embrace Change* (2nd ed.). Addison-Wesley.
- Campbell, E., Schmidt, E., Rosenberg, J., & Eagle, A. (2019). *Trillion Dollar Coach: The Leadership Playbook of Silicon Valley's Bill Campbell*. Harper Business.
- Covey, S. R. (1989). *The 7 Habits of Highly Effective People*. Free Press.
- Cohn, M. (2004). *User Stories Applied: For Agile Software Development*. Addison-Wesley.
- Deloitte. (2023). *Continuous Improvement in the Project Economy*. Deloitte Insights.
- Drucker, P. F. (2001). *The Essential Drucker*. HarperBusiness.
- Forbes. (2022). "Micro-Pivots vs. Macro-Pivots: How Small Adjustments Drive Strategic Agility." *Forbes Magazine*.
- Gartner. (2023). *Adaptive Delivery: Embedding Incremental Change in Enterprise PMOs*. Gartner Inc.
- Goldratt, E. M. (1997). *Critical Chain*. North River Press.
- Harvard Business Review. (2022). "Small Bets: How Continuous Iteration Beats Big Transformations." *Harvard Business Review*.
- Iacocca, L. (1984). *Iacocca: An Autobiography*. Bantam Books.
- Iacocca, L. (2007). *Where Have All the Leaders Gone?* Scribner.
- Isaacson, W. (2011). *Steve Jobs*. Simon & Schuster.
- Jocko Willink & Babin, L. (2015). Extreme Ownership: *How U.S. Navy SEALs Lead and Win*. St. Martin's Press.

- Kogon, K., Blakemore, S., & Wood, J. (2015). *Project Management for the Unofficial Project Manager*. BenBella Books.
- McChrystal, S. (2015). *Team of Teams: New Rules of Engagement for a Complex World*. Penguin.
- McKinsey & Company. (2023). *The Power of Incremental Change: Driving Transformation Through Micro-Pivots*. McKinsey Global Institute.
- Meredith, J. R., Shafer, S. M., & Mantel, S. J. (2017). *Project Management: A Managerial Approach* (10th ed.). Wiley.
- PMI (Project Management Institute). (2021). *A Guide to the Project Management Body of Knowledge (PMBOK® Guide) – Seventh Edition*. Project Management Institute.
- PMI. (2017). *Agile Practice Guide*. Project Management Institute.
- Ries, E. (2011). *The Lean Startup*. Crown Business.
- Ries, E. (2017). *The Startup Way*. Currency.
- Scrum.org. (2022). "Agile Leadership and Micro-Pivots in Practice." *Scrum.org Blog*.
- Sutherland, J. (2014). *Scrum: The Art of Doing Twice the Work in Half the Time*. Crown Business.
- Tapscott, D., & Tapscott, A. (2016). *Blockchain Revolution*. Penguin.
- Walsh, B. (2009). *The Score Takes Care of Itself: My Philosophy of Leadership*. Portfolio.
- Winnona Partners. (2021). "How YouTube's Early Micro-Pivots Shaped Its Success." *Winnona Partners Blog*.
- Startup Savant. (2021). "The Slack Pivot: From Glitch to Global Communications Platform." *Startup Savant*.
- Nicolagraham. (2022). "The Power of Micro-Pivots." *Issue No. 56*. Substack.

CHAPTER 19

- Altucher, J. (2013). *Choose Yourself: Be Happy, Make Millions, Live the Dream*. Lioncrest Publishing.
- Blanchard, K., & Johnson, S. (1989). *The One Minute Manager Meets the Monkey*. HarperCollins.
- Campbell, E., Schmidt, E., Rosenberg, J., & Eagle, A. (2019). *Trillion Dollar Coach: The Leadership Playbook of Silicon Valley's Bill Campbell*. Harper Business.
- Covey, S. R. (1989). *The 7 Habits of Highly Effective People*. Free Press.

- Drucker, P. F. (2001). *The Essential Drucker: The Best of Sixty Years of Peter Drucker's Essential Writings on Management.* HarperBusiness.
- Iacocca, L. (1984). *Iacocca: An Autobiography.* Bantam Books.
- Kerzner, H. (2022). *Project Management: A Systems Approach to Planning, Scheduling, and Controlling* (13th ed.). Wiley.
- Kerzner, H. (2019). *Innovation Project Management.* Wiley.
- Kogon, K., Blakemore, S., & Wood, J. (2015). *Project Management for the Unofficial Project Manager.* FranklinCovey.
- Meredith, J. R., Shafer, S. M., & Mantel, S. J. (2017). *Project Management: A Managerial Approach* (10th ed.). Wiley.
- PMI (Project Management Institute). (2021). *A Guide to the Project Management Body of Knowledge* (PMBOK® Guide) – Seventh Edition. Project Management Institute.
- Prosci. (2022). *Best Practices in Change Management Benchmarking Report.* Prosci Inc.
- NASA Ames Research Center, NAS Division PMO. (2020–2025). *Internal PMO Templates and Governance Documents.* NASA Ames Research Center.

CHAPTER 20

- Altucher, J. (2013). *Choose Yourself: Be Happy, Make Millions, Live the Dream.* Lioncrest Publishing.
- Covey, S. R. (1989). *The 7 Habits of Highly Effective People.* Free Press.
- Drucker, P. F. (2001). *The Essential Drucker.* HarperBusiness.
- Iacocca, L. (1984). *Iacocca: An Autobiography.* Bantam Books.
- Kerzner, H. (2022). *Project Management: A Systems Approach to Planning, Scheduling, and Controlling* (13th ed.). Wiley.
- Peterson, J. B. (2018). *12 Rules for Life: An Antidote to Chaos.* Random House Canada.
- Peterson, J. B. (2021). *Beyond Order: 12 More Rules for Life.* Penguin Books.
- PMI (Project Management Institute). (2021). *A Guide to the Project Management Body of Knowledge (PMBOK® Guide) –* Seventh Edition. Project Management Institute.
- U.S. Bureau of Labor Statistics. (2024). *Employee Benefits Survey.* U.S. Department of Labor.
- Kaiser Family Foundation. (2024). *Employer Health Benefits Survey.*

- Howe, N. (2023). *The Fourth Turning Is Here: What the Seasons of History Tell Us About How and When This Crisis Will End.* Simon & Schuster.
- Howe, N., & Strauss, W. (1997). *The Fourth Turning: An American Prophecy.* Broadway Books.

www.ingramcontent.com/pod-product-compliance
Lightning Source LLC
Chambersburg PA
CBHW051732250726
48659CB00001B/26